FOR YOU.

♡ MARY x

The Popular Girls

Helping Your Daughter with Adolescent Power Struggles

7 Steps for Flourishing

Dr Mary Kaspar

First published by Ultimate World Publishing 2022
Copyright © 2022 Dr Mary Kaspar

ISBN

Paperback: 978-1-922714-45-9
Ebook: 978-1-922714-46-6

Cover design: Ultimate World Publishing
Layout and typesetting: Ultimate World Publishing
Editor: Marinda Wilkinson
Photography: Simon Scott

Ultimate World Publishing
Diamond Creek,
Victoria Australia 3089
www.writeabook.com.au

The paper in this book is FSC® certified.
FSC® promotes environmentally responsible,
socially beneficial and economically viable
management of the world's forests.

Praise for

The Popular Girls

'This is an outstanding book. It's the most thorough I have ever seen on this subject. It is also strong on answers – ways that you can help your daughter choose to be kind, and develop her values and goals for how she will treat people throughout her life. Mary Kaspar has been deeply involved in helping girls over many years and knows their world, and their pain, inside out. And she knows how to fix it.'

– STEVE BIDDULPH, author of *Raising Boys, Raising Girls* and *10 Things Girls Need Most*

'*The Popular Girls* provides a seven-step guide towards the type of popularity science links to success. This includes a range of new approaches to overcoming obstacles often found in adolescent relationships. Dr Mary Kaspar writes with experience and from the heart as a sister and mother to three daughters. She shows through examples that learning healthy ways of interacting includes bringing compassion and kindness even to difficult situations.'

– SHARON SALZBERG, author of *Lovingkindness, Real Change* and the New York Times Bestseller *Real Happiness*

'Mary Kaspar shares her clinical and educational expertise in this compelling book which unpacks the complexity of "popularity" in girls. Covering timely topics such as social media, Kaspar also writes about aspects of relational aggression that have been previously overlooked: the role of teachers and schools, family values and the influence of romantic relationships. This book should be helpful to a diverse audience of parents, teachers and girls.'

– CHERYL DELLASEGA, professor, Pennsylvania State University, author of *Girl Grudges: Learning How to Forgive and Live, Girl Wars: 12 Strategies That Will End Female Bullying, Surviving Ophelia* and founder of Club and Camp Ophelia

'As a researcher in the area of positive psychology and as the mother of a daughter, I find the content of this book inspiring. Dr Kaspar describes social and personal challenges and dilemmas faced by girls that will be familiar to many teens, parents and educators. She offers approaches and strategies that are based on research as well as her own experiences that assist girls in overcoming these challenges.'

– NICOLA SCHUTTE, associate professor of psychology, University of New England and co-author of *Activities to Enhance Social, Emotional, and Problem-Solving Skills: Ninety Activities that Teach Children, Adolescents, and Adults Skills Crucial to Success in Life*

'In an easy-to-read narrative style, this insightful book outlines and highlights key aspects about girls and their relationships with each other, which at times, can be fraught with conflict and tension. Mary has written a great resource that presents a way forward in simple, timely and powerful steps. It is a book that parents will definitely want to share with each other and with their daughters. It's a well-researched and practical guide that addresses girls' aggression and replace these serious and detrimental behaviours with positive core values.'

– ANGELA PAGE, senior lecturer, School of Education,
University of Newcastle

'This book is an erudite balance of research, clinical skills, and personal experience, leading to a very impressive collection of sensible and professional insights.'

– DAVID HORGAN, clinical associate professor of
psychiatry, University of Melbourne, previous senior specialist,
Royal Melbourne Hospital and founder of Australian Suicide
Prevention Foundation

'This little book is fantastic! I devoured it in one sitting, and kept thinking, "If only I had had this book when . . . ". *The Popular Girls* is a first of its kind. It provides an illuminating and well-constructed road map that will instil confidence in your ability to help your clients, your daughter, and even your sons, navigate a skilful, kind and compassionate course through the trickiest terrain of adolescent peer relationships. The book makes theory and research findings easy to understand, and the synthesis of a huge literature is distilled into a rich and systematic framework that navigates wide-ranging territory seamlessly. At the same time it is redolent with the personal journey of a deeply committed therapist and mother, Dr Mary Kaspar.'

– CAROLINE CROFT, clinical psychologist, founder of
The Centre for Equanimity

To my daughters, Ash, Gabi and Georgia

CONTENTS

FOREWORD

A time of challenge, a time of growth, a time during which characteristics that influence her journey into and through adulthood develop; these are hallmarks of a girl's adolescence. In this book, Dr Mary Kaspar takes the reader into the sometimes confronting world of girls' teenage years. She offers insights regarding the social and personal challenges faced by girls and provides valuable practical advice on how parents can assist girls in dealing with these challenges and in developing resilience and lifelong skills for the type of popularity linked to wellbeing.

I have known Dr Kaspar for a number of years. I worked with her on her doctoral research, which focused on socially anxious children's perception of threat and how changing these perceptions, by considering a number of explanations, may alleviate anxiety. Since that time, a significant portion of Dr Kaspar's therapy work has focused on assisting children and adolescents facing problems. Her long-term passion for assisting children and adolescents, her academic qualifications, her insights from therapy work and her perspectives as a mother of daughters provide foundations for the content of this book.

As a researcher in the area of positive psychology and as the mother of a daughter, I find the content of the book inspiring. Dr Kaspar describes social and personal challenges and dilemmas faced by girls that will be familiar to many teens, parents and educators. She offers approaches and strategies that are based on research as well as her own experiences that assist girls in overcoming these challenges. Many of these approaches are grounded in positive psychology, which focuses on the recognition and development of strengths. Dr Kaspar provides insights into how to encourage characteristics such as connectedness with others, finding meaning, gratitude, developing mindfulness and identifying individual signature strengths. The building of these characteristics helps girls to flourish.

As Dr Kaspar points out, girls are limitless. Parents of girls, as well as boys (as some of the challenges and development of skills covered also apply to boys) will find that the themes of the book resonate with them. Educators, and teens themselves, will also find the book engaging and meaningful. When applied, Dr Kaspar's approaches will assist children in flourishing and developing that limitless potential that is closely linked to the characteristics of likeable popularity.

Nicola Schutte
Associate Professor of Psychology, University of New England

INTRODUCTION

Girls are my world.

Growing up, I had four sisters close in age, and I have been blessed with three daughters. I love being around girls and the exciting conversations that arise. Time with adolescents is often full of fun, laughter and happiness. Young people embrace life at a rapid pace and with such enthusiasm as they explore and see the world with fresh insight and vitality. Girls' friendships are a large part of what makes adolescence so vibrant. Together, the generated energy and enthusiasm are contagious and can diminish seemingly insurmountable problems. Meaningful and satisfying friendships interact and amplify with other components of wellbeing such as positive emotions, engagement, meaning and accomplishment. Together girls flourish.

The adolescent social arena corresponds with developmental changes in the brain resulting in girls wanting to spend more time with friends, being more sensitive to rejection and prioritising peer affiliations. It is rewarding to see girls happy in their friendships, but equally heartbreaking when they end in conflict. As parents, we love our daughters and never want to see them unhappy. A mother once told me that she was only ever as happy as her least happy child, a sentiment that reflects how deeply we as parents can share our girls' distress. Whilst we would like to shield our daughters from the discomfort of friendship problems and social difficulties, this is not always possible nor advisable. Challenges can contribute to some of our daughter's most significant learnings, and our role as parents is to guide her towards learning the right lessons when relationships become frayed.

If you are reading this book, you have probably tried numerous ways to help your daughter successfully navigate her social world. You may have told her to treat others nicely and reassured her that it was not important that she was left out from being invited to that party. You may have laid out guidelines around social media use and encouraged her to do her best to ignore hurtful comments. Yet, despite your best efforts, you may find that there are not always easy answers or quick fixes to social challenges. *The Popular Girls* is designed to support the parents and adults who would like their daughter or the girls they care about to flourish during adolescence. We can't overlook the critical role that relationships play in girls' development and their ability to succeed.

My commitment to helping girls learn the right skills for healthy relationships started over 15 years ago and laid the foundation for *The Popular Girls*. In approximately 2007, I was teaching in the clinical child psychology program at the University of New England and created a group program for girls run as part of my psychology practice. This program was referred to in general terms as resilience skills. It was a natural progression from the 'Smart and Social' research I conducted for my doctoral thesis. In the resilience skills program, the evidence-based skills contributing to good emotional and social health were mapped out as was known to be best practice.

My experience is that girls benefit from building strong skills in active problem-solving, communicating, regulating emotions and balancing thoughts. Together, these skills are time tested for improving symptoms of anxiety and depression and can provide a buffer for common adolescent social stressors. Importantly, adolescence is also a time for increasing independence for self-care. Developing healthy habits for regular exercise, balanced nutrition and a good sleep routine can improve girls' wellbeing tremendously. Over the years, I refined the techniques and processes for teaching evidence-based skills in practical and fun ways.

I have learnt so much from observing and talking with girls in my practice. My understanding has been extended by conversations with girls' parents, colleagues who care about girls and the growing research. As a parent of daughters, I have gained another perspective on girls' social lives, including their interactions with boys, their role as students and their engagement with broader cultural messages. When considering social conflict, greater depth and clarity is gained by knowledge about the complex role of social cruelty and peer popularity. *The Popular Girls* adds another piece to the adolescent social puzzle by looking more closely at the power of popularity to change adolescent preferences, values and behaviours.

Although we look through the lens of gender, it is likely that some of the guidance provided also helps with raising sons, as boys too struggle with the social dynamics of school. Understanding particular difficulties confronting our youth is helpful; however, it is not the same as knowing what we can do to address problems.

Whilst the emergence of the increasing importance of popularity during adolescence is not new, some things are changing for our daughters more than our sons. There is a gender imbalance in stress symptoms during adolescence, with emotional problems increasingly affecting girls more significantly than boys. Underlying the increasing emergence of girls anxious and depressive symptoms are several discrepancies. Girls are more negatively affected by mistreatment from their peers and exposure to the internet and social media. Our youth live in an unprecedented age of access to digital technology where they are bombarded by messages promoting an increasing focus on the self. Girls are more likely to feel pressure about their physical appearance and academic performance. These stressors impact the emotional health of our daughters and their social interactions.

The Popular Girls highlights the importance of relationships for our daughters' emotional and physical health and explores the role of social dominance and popularity in peer social interactions. Chapter by chapter, the social behaviours associated with social dominance orientations are unpacked, including the role of relational aggression. Relational aggression can change for the worse during future social interactions between the girls engaging in the abusive behaviour and their targets. However, without knowing what to look for, these damaging behaviours can happen right in front of us without acknowledgement.

This book does more than uncover factors harming the formation of healthy relationships. It also provides suggestions for guiding our daughters towards the type of popularity that science says is linked to success. Our daughters' ability to act with courage and compassion and to develop authentic connections with others are the cornerstones of thriving.

While I have explained some concepts with examples, these examples have been altered, with several comprising composites of more than one story. The information has been changed and identifying details removed to maintain confidentiality. An exception is the leadership insights and comments shared by my sister Katherine.

The Popular Girls aims to take a comprehensive look at adolescent popularity challenges and open a range of new approaches to overcoming relationship obstacles. We can do a great deal to help girls feel more connected and effective in facing challenges we know will come their way. At times, when you are reading the examples illustrated, you may identify with the lessons. The experiences that apply to school situations are also relevant to social dynamics later in life. Ways of interacting with others can be learned and transferred into adulthood.

In this book, are many suggestions to assist our daughters with miswantings and relational aggression. In Part 1, the types, layers and complexities of popularity are described, along with the effect they have on the wellbeing and development of our girls. Part 2 is where you'll find my seven-step road map that will help you guide your girls towards healthy relationships, likeable popularity and a limitless future.

Let's get started!

POPULARITY:
The Good, the Not-So-Good and Everything In-Between

Friends Matter!

This is the world I want to live in. The shared world.
– NAOMI SHIHAB NYE

Humans are innately social and young people have high social needs. Girls learn with their friends and grow with their friends. A girl's ability to form healthy and satisfying relationships is also linked to her future happiness and health – and even her lifespan. For this reason, it makes sense to care about your daughter's friendships a lot.

Social changes during adolescence are related to adjustments in the development of the brain. The period of adolescence broadly encompasses the age range from 12 to 24 years, marking the developmental period between childhood and adulthood. During this time, the brain matures at an uneven pace as it remodels. The back of the brain develops first. This includes the limbic system, which is the oldest part of the brain. It is involved in the experience of intense emotions and risk-taking behaviour. The prefrontal cortex, which exerts control over a girl's impulses, lags in development. Girls will naturally look for opportunities for expansion, novelty and social engagement outside of the family. Adolescence represents a critical time for social development, including increased learning about caring for others and receiving care in return. These years are a time when girls' skills for initiating and maintaining healthy relationships can be refined.

Adolescent girls care about being with friends a lot. In my house, the COVID-19 pandemic highlighted this. I have three daughters, although only one still lived at home when the lockdown orders were put in place. My youngest daughter, Georgia, went to great lengths to convince me to bend the rules, which prevented her from leaving home to visit friends. One evening in June, she even tried to slip out the door without me noticing.

'Please, you don't understand,' Georgia pleaded with me.

Georgia was still a student when the pandemic started. She had been participating in classes from home for several weeks and was missing face-to-face catch-ups with her friends. Georgia presented a well-argued plan for visiting Beau. Instead of entering Beau's house, she would sit on outdoor furniture in the cold and dark, separated by 1.5 metres. She would wear a mask and use hand sanitiser before leaving and before returning home. Unfortunately, at the time, even this plan violated the stay-at-home orders.

COVID-19 lockdowns highlighted many of the social freedoms we had taken for granted. Despite Georgia thinking I did not understand, I did know that her instinct to be with her friends was healthy and normal. I felt terrible that she was missing out on something so important to her. Whilst spending time with her family at home was great, it could not offset the benefits from her spending time with good friends. Georgia was at the age during which she was moving towards increasing relatedness with her peers and interdependence with her family. Interdependence describes a young person's need to remain connected whilst navigating the world more independently. As parents, we can think about the concept of interdependence as flying lessons. Girls still need to return to their parents for frequent landings after they first learn to fly. These landings allow them to draw on a valued source of wisdom to help them keep safe and make the right decisions. The landings become less frequent as their experiences and skills grow.

Georgia's desire to be with her friend was helpful. Doing fun things with our friends rather than doing those same things on our own is a smart move. A Yale University study conducted by Boothby and colleagues found that sharing positive experiences with someone else amplifies the experience compared to doing the same activity without someone else. For example, chocolate eaten with a friend becomes more 'likeable and flavourful' than eating it alone. Friends make fun activities even more fun, increasing positive emotion.

The benefits provided by good friendships also extends to improving girls' mental health. Liked and included youth are protected from anxious and depressive symptoms compared to youth without friends. These youth experience better academic performance and productivity. Friends also contribute significantly to increasing social skills and problem-solving. The more a young person interacts positively with others, the more advanced and sophisticated their skills become in sharing and negotiating conflicts. These skills, in turn, improve a young person's friendships. The process is cyclic; girls with good friendships will be more likely to have good friendships in the future.

Friendships have the power to improve a girl's experience of adversity. When people experience distressing social situations, the brain activates in similar ways to the experience of physical pain. During our evolution, belonging to a tribe provided physical protection, shelter and food. Social pain is a warning signal that all is not well. Our biological system responds not only to social stressors but to social support. When a girl speaks with a good friend after a stressful social incident, her regulation of cortisol, the stress hormone, can improve. Talking through problems and having the support of friends provides a girl with comfort and impacts a girl's immune system in healing ways. Relationships influence biological systems and good relationships confer benefits to girls' physical health.

Martin Seligman, a leader in the field of positive psychology, emphasises good relationships as one of five building blocks for flourishing. Healthy, successful flourishing is more than simple happiness or the absence of illness. Instead, it is about growth and thriving. The other four building blocks of flourishing are positive emotion, engagement related to the experience of flow, meaning through belonging to something bigger than oneself and accomplishment or achievement. Relationships interact with the other building blocks of flourishing, adding to and receiving from the components in a dynamic process.

The outcomes from a significant longitudinal study further highlight the importance of relationships for psychological and physical health. The Harvard Grant Study started in 1938, with researchers following more than 700 people from adolescence over 75 years. The study initially thought that biological determinism, including physical constitution and intellectual ability, would best predict successful aging. By the end of the study, it was the presence of healthy relationships that were the most crucial factors for a successful life. On average, those with ratings of warm and intimate relationships experienced delays in deterioration of their mental and physical health and lived longer, happier lives. The effect of relationships was stronger than social class, intelligence and genetics. Social ties were more important to happiness than working hard, money or fame. Conversely, in the words of the fourth program director Robert Waldinger, 'loneliness kills'.

LONELINESS

So, what is loneliness? The Australian Psychological Society describes loneliness as a 'feeling of distress people experience when their social relations are not the way they would like'. For several years now, research has pointed towards loneliness as a looming health problem. Loneliness in youth is linked to poorer general health, increased medical visits, impaired sleep and poorer emotional regulation. In 2019, Michelle Lim and associates reported on the Young Australian Loneliness Survey which involved 1500 youth. They found problematic levels of loneliness affect one in six 12 to 17-year-olds and one in three 18 to 25-year-olds. Of the adolescents surveyed, 43 per cent feel alone 'sometimes' or 'always', 50 per cent lack companionship 'sometimes' or 'always' and feel left out 'sometimes' or 'always', and 52 per cent feel close to two or fewer friends that they can call on for help.

Contact with others and inclusion matters. During the COVID-19 pandemic, surveys highlighted how forced social restrictions and isolation increased the experience of social disconnection and loneliness for many people, with one in two people reporting they felt more lonely. As a result, the prevalence of anxious and depressive symptoms significantly increased. For those already experiencing anxiety or depression, mental health symptoms further deteriorated. The impact of COVID-19 restrictions is predicted to persist even after restrictions are lifted, with the health toll expected to be felt for some time.

Loneliness is not only about being in contact with others; it also involves a personal feeling of social isolation. These constructs are independent. A young person can be surrounded by others but still be lonely or can spend time alone but not feel lonely. It may be that many girls who, on the surface, seem to be embedded in the social structures of school and family still experience loneliness.

Adolescence comprises one of two risk periods for loneliness. The transition through adolescence and young adulthood involves rapid physical and psychological changes and presents a vulnerable period for relationship difficulties. It is a time of increased learning of sophisticated social principles, friendship skills and evaluations of relationships. Changing emotions around social interactions involve a heightened sensitivity to social evaluations and strong emotional reactions to misunderstandings and disagreements with friends. A girl must deal with needs for autonomy and relatedness as she strives to find a unique identity and turns to her peer group for belonging.

Adolescence is also when some girls are experiencing the emergence of mental health problems, including anxiety and depressive symptoms. In general, girls report feeling more stress symptoms related to academic performance and appearance than boys. Girls are also more emotionally affected by social cruelty from their peers. While stress itself is not inherently harmful to girls, stress becomes unhealthy when the demands on a girl exceed the resources available to address the problem, such as time, support and knowledge.

Adolescence is also a time of exceptional opportunity. It is an inflection point with developmental implications. Whilst it is heartbreaking to see our daughters suffer, the experience of social difficulties can present opportunities for developing coping skills for managing conflict, preparing girls for more challenging future problems. When developing the right skills and extending their capabilities, girls can be reminded that they are tougher than they realise.

My awareness of adolescence as a unique window of opportunity was the precursor for creating a skills building group program for girls run from my clinical psychology practice. Girls have the potential to learn how to improve their emotional and social health and at a speedy pace. There are many benefits from girls learning and practising skills for self-care such as exercise, nutrition and sleep habits and dealing with social challenges using goal setting, assertive communication, thought balancing and mindfulness. The efficacy of these interventions is well established. Researcher David Dunning and his colleagues conducted a meta-analysis of data from over 3,500 youths collected across 33 studies. They found that mindfulness-based programs improve cognitive functioning, depression, anxiety and negative behaviours.

Adding to these programs, strategies that may help reduce loneliness tend to improve how a young person expresses openness to being friends with others and positive emotions. Our daughters' ability to make and maintain friendships improves with solid skills for good emotion regulation and distress tolerance. Increasing prosocial behaviours and sharing positive experiences with peers can also help upregulate positive emotions and downregulate negative emotions. A girl can develop skills to think positively about social situations, be a good listener and tolerate the discomfort of socially awkward situations.

Loneliness is not restricted to adolescence. Many adults struggle to establish and maintain healthy relationships. Why can relationships be so hard? In the words of Robert Waldinger from the Harvard Grant Study, 'relationships are messy and they're complicated'. The concept of having good relationships is abstract and broad. What exactly is a good relationship? How do you meet the expectations for happy and healthy relationships? What are the obstacles? These are all critical questions.

When looking for answers to these questions, we can turn to the wisdom of those who have lived full lives and the insights they obtained from reflecting on their past experiences. What do people say at the end of their life that they wished they had done differently? Bronnie Ware, a palliative care nurse and author of the book *The Top Five Regrets of the Dying*, describes how people's regrets are often about spending time on distractions, which, although seemingly minor, can build over time to become significant life missteps. These missteps took them away from their meaningful relationships. People wished they had spent more time with those they cared about and shared their authentic feelings and thoughts, rather than following others' expectations. The wisdom of experience sorted the essential from the rest, but it appears that this insight comes too late in life for many. We can help our daughters learn these important lessons earlier in life. We can acknowledge distractions that take girls away from healthy and authentic relationships.

SUMMARY OF KEY POINTS

- Friendships are important during adolescence for wellbeing and learning.

- Connecting with others in healthy ways during adolescence has the potential to set girls on a trajectory of success in multiple areas of her life.

- We can encourage and support girls to 'lean in' to existing connections and 'reach out' for new connections.

The Two Faces of Popularity

What is right is not always popular, and what is popular is not always right.

– ALBERT EINSTEIN

Our daughters' ability to connect with others in warm and healthy ways can predict their success in multiple aspects of their lives. As parents, we want our daughters to achieve this success and are most likely prepared to put in time and effort to support them.

Adolescence is a period when girls care a lot about what their peers think of them. Should we support our daughter's focus on others' opinions and judgements? Adolescents care about fitting in with their classmates. Should we encourage our daughters to do what it takes to fit in? During this developmental period, girls tend to want a lot of friends. How many friends does a girl need?

Is our daughter on the right track if she is popular at school?

Whether we were popular in high school and the level of popularity achieved, seems to matter, even long after high school is over. The tendency for popularity memories to be replayed over and over and take on meaning has captured my attention several times.

One of these times was when I was working in neuropsychology early in my career.

Before administering test batteries, I would conduct a clinical interview to gather information about a person's history and the reasons for the testing. This information would guide the tests chosen and add to the overall understanding of the test outcomes. I would always finish the interview by asking whether there was anything important that I had forgotten to ask. On this particular day, Mrs Tierney, a 60-year-old married office manager, responded to my question with an unusual answer.

'I was in the popular group at school,' Mrs Tierney said.

Mrs Tierney was well-groomed and neatly dressed, wearing understated jewellery and a merino cardigan, with excellent posture. She held my gaze with confidence and I detected a slight look of pride flash across her face. I paused to gather my thoughts and wrote down her response whilst she observed.

'Why does she want me to know this?' I thought. I tossed around the idea of what it meant to be popular in senior school and how this might be relevant to Mrs Tierney's neuropsychological assessment. What was certain was that Mrs Tierney perceived her popularity in high school to be a positive achievement.

I was sitting in a final senior school assembly many years later when Mrs Tierney's reference to popularity again came to mind. I was part of a large audience listening to a senior officer from the Defence Force address the graduating students. The hot weather and the packed hall of students and parents tended to make end-of-year ceremonies claustrophobic, resulting in the audience fanning themselves with their booklets. Regardless, the senior officer's address captivated the audience, as she wove engaging stories of adventures at home and overseas with essential life lessons. She had achieved great things in the Defence Force and was an inspiring role model, demonstrating perseverance and courage to pursue her inclinations in her career to great success.

She ended her address with a final message to the students. 'When I was sitting where you are now', she paused and stared intently at the rows of students seated before her, 'I was *not* in the popular group.'

Herein lies a problem. The answer to how important popularity is for your daughter depends on how popularity is defined. Some people attribute popularity as a marker of success, yet others attribute their success to *not* being popular.

DECONSTRUCTING POPULARITY

According to the Cambridge Dictionary, 'popular' means to be liked, enjoyed or supported by many people. Based on this definition, it is reasonable to think that popularity is great. However, how peers determine popularity in adolescence indicates that the term popularity is more complicated than it first appears. When we deconstruct popularity, two different concepts emerge, yet only one is predictive of future success. So, the answer to whether popularity is important is both yes and no.

At a young age, children tend to describe those peers who they like the most as popular. These popular children are typically described as agreeable, cooperative, happy and good at sharing, following the rules, having reciprocal conversations and solving social problems. Children will also nominate a second group of their peers who are liked by some and equally disliked by others. These children are referred to as controversial.

During adolescence, being nominated as liked by peers remains one type of popularity, referred to as 'likeable popularity'. These youth connect well with others and tend to be on the developmental trajectory of initiating and maintaining healthy relationships. Likeable popularity describes those adolescents that make others feel safe and good about themselves. But likeable popularity is not the type of popularity we think of when we hear the word popular. When adolescents are asked which peers are most popular, instead of being asked which peers they like the most, the second type of popularity, referred to as 'status popularity', emerges. The status popular adolescents are more like the group of peers in childhood referred to as controversial. Most girls with high likeable popularity are low in status popularity. Popularity in adolescence has two faces.

Adolescents commonly describe status popular girls as cool, nice, funny, daring, exciting, confident, socially appropriate, socially central, accepted and included by the group, influential, fashionable, well-groomed, conceited, exclusionary and mean. This combination of descriptors may seem contradictory; being nice and being mean are often thought of on two ends of the spectrum of prosocial and antisocial behaviour. Psychological science and popular culture such as the *Mean Girls* film and *Gossip Girl* TV series show both behaviours can be present at high levels.

The word 'bistrategic' identifies the combination of these two distinctly different types of behaviours as strategies for social dominance, as described in Patricia Hawley's evolutionary-based Resource Control Theory. To meet the criterion, a ranking above the 66th percentile of prosocial behaviours *and* coercive behaviours in comparison to peers is required. Bistrategic resource controllers are most likely to be status popular youth, and according to recent studies, generally make up approximately 15 per cent of the peer group, although this percentage varies.

Bistrategic resource control is also observed in other social primates when competing for physical, social and sexual resources. Despite the evolutionary connection, the quest for status popularity is partly rooted in our Western culture. Youth that uses aggression in Western countries, with an individualistic focus, tend to obtain popularity and admiration. In contrast, youth who use aggression in more collectivist countries tend to lose popularity.

Simply put, the bistrategic strategy involves getting along to get ahead. It is the use of selective and difficult to detect aggression, often balanced with highly visible and skilled prosocial behaviours, that result in high general peer and adult regard. Bistrategic resource controllers are also referred to as Machiavellian, which describes a personality construct involving manipulativeness. Bistrategic resource controllers are the most successful at dominating and controlling the peer group and determining an individual girl's inclusion and social esteem.

The differences between likeable and status popular girls seem evident in both behaviours and emerging personality characteristics. Tests of personality traits, including a 2020 study by researcher Reinout E de Vries and associates, indicate that likeable popular youth tend to obtain higher ratings on measures of openness to experience, agreeableness, honesty, humility, fairness and modesty, and lower ratings for greed, compared to status popular youth. These differences in traits suggest that status popularity is associated with having higher opinions of oneself and being prepared to take more than others and what is fair.

Underlying the two faces of popularity seems to be fundamental differences in the way that relationships are viewed. The differences can be compared to a field and a staircase. Likeable popularity, also referred to as likeability, involves walking alongside others. Imagine a large, flat, green field stretching out before you, with lots of space for everyone. Many different people are walking in the area; there are people to your left and your right. Some are moving forward and some move forward behind them and in front of them. The distance covered and walking speed differs between people. The people are not the same, but they are considered equal on their journey and walk together as companions.

In contrast, some people view others in competition for scarce resources. This could be conceptualised as people ascending a flight of stairs. Imagine there is a long flight of stairs reaching another level above you. People are standing on every level of the stairs. Some people are higher on the stairs and some people are lower. Only a fixed number of people can fit on any one level, so to ascend the stairs, you need to find a way of changing positions with someone above you and at the same time, you need to make sure that someone below you cannot pull you down and take your place. This scarcity mindset involves a hyperawareness of what is lacking and where we stand in relation to others. Scarcity involves fear about not having enough or not being enough. The bistrategic strategies of being cool and cruel are competitive tools for standing higher on the stairs.

COERCIVE BEHAVIOURS

Coercive strategies, or being cruel, is a way to obtain resources by harming or threatening another person's wellbeing. Aggression can be separated into several different forms. Overt aggression often involves physical and verbal attacks and is easier to identify and respond to as it is more visible. In comparison, relational aggression involves behaviours designed to damage and manipulate social relationships, such as spreading rumours and intentional exclusion. Relational aggression may create just as much or more harm to a person as physical aggression. A 2020 review of 46 studies conducted by Assistant Professor Deborah Casper and her colleagues, analysed data gathered from over 35,000 adolescents. They found that peer-rated popular youth most commonly perpetrate relational aggression. This relational aggression is covert and easily missed by peers and teachers.

How do cruel behaviours play out in the peer group? Below is a list of relationally aggressive behaviours:

- Purposefully excluding or leaving out a girl from a social event or activity
- Threatening to withdraw friendship
- Deliberately refusing to speak to a girl or making negative facial expressions directed at a girl
- Passing on rumours or gossip that damage a girl's reputation
- Refusing to sit near a girl in class or at lunch
- Making derogatory comments about a girl's character
- Making fun of a girl
- Controlling the behaviours of the group to exclude a girl.

Aggressive behaviour can also be differentiated as proactive or reactive. Proactive aggression, also termed 'cold-blooded', is most effective at increasing status popularity and is more commonly used in bistrategic resource control. It is described as actions which are:

- Unprovoked
- Deliberate
- Occurs with an absence of anger or distress
- Instrumental in achieving personal gains such as domination or intimidation
- Internally driven with reward focus.

In contrast, reactive aggression, also referred to as 'hot-blooded', is described as:

- A defensive or retaliatory response to perceived threat or provocation
- Accompanied by emotions such as anger or frustration
- Impulsive
- Aimed at reducing fear, anger or stress.

Adolescents can show both types of aggression, including within a single scenario. For example, a girl who is caught out using proactive aggression may not like being criticised and retaliate with reactive aggression. Whereas a target of bullying may demonstrate reactive aggression due to distress.

PROSOCIAL BEHAVIOURS

Prosocial strategies, or being cool, can be used to successfully obtain more social resources and alliances by focusing on positive relationships. Prosocial behaviours include agreeable, conscientious, attuned, responsive, fair, kind, reciprocal, cooperative, helpful, sympathetic, positive and respectful behaviours. Dominant youth understand that being liked is essential for success and can be highly socially perceptive, empathetic and morally astute. Prosocial strategies consider the needs and desires of others by fostering cooperative and loyal relationships, making oneself indispensable and rewarding. Consequently, prosocial strategies help girls achieve individual benefits, including group approval.

Girls interested in social dominance will often choose to affiliate themselves with other socially dominant peers, including adolescents who use bistrategic strategies or predominantly use prosocial methods for status, also referred to as prosocial resource control. Being a part of a socially dominant group offers many advantages, including access to resources for enjoyment and protection that girls can't acquire or defend alone. This is not to say that there will not be competition within the group, as the social group itself is a source of competition for the very resources it facilitates. In general, however, the specific techniques used in bistrategic control will differ based on the context, with different control methods for peers within the group and peers outside the group.

Although some girls use prosocial behaviours because they care about others, it is reasonable to assume that some girls use prosocial strategies to obtain status popularity and special treatment. Therefore, prosocial behaviours in some situations act like a 'cloak of presentation'. Whilst it is appropriate for our daughters to take pride in their presentation and show social etiquette, it is important to understand that an excessive focus on appearances to control another's perception is a dysfunctional way of engaging with others.

The Turkish story of a 13th century religious leader named Nasreddin Hoca illustrates how outward presentations tell us very little about a person. Hoca is invited to a banquet in a neighbouring city but did not have time to change his clothing before the occasion and, upon arrival, was overlooked by the host. Once Hoca changed into a fine striking coat and returned, the host responded more favourably, providing him with preferential treatment. Hoca realised that people were responding to his outward attire and not to him. Was it his fine coat that was more important than him? As the dinner progressed, Hoca began stuffing his food into the pockets of his coat, exclaiming, 'Eat, my fine coat!' After all, it was Hoca's fine coat that was the guest of honour.

THE POPULARITY PARADOX

Girls are especially motivated to obtain status popularity during adolescence. Increases in status popularity result in dopamine and oxytocin in brain regions such as the ventral striatum, associated with reward processing and pleasure. The cortex of the adolescent brain doesn't mature until the mid-twenties, at which time strivings for status becomes better restrained or balanced. However, concerns about status tend to effect all of us not only during adolescence, but to varying extents over our lifespan.

Mitch Prinstein, clinical psychologist and expert on popularity, highlights the popularity paradox. Whereas a girl's instincts and urges direct her to crave status popularity; it is likeable popularity that will contribute to her social wellbeing and flourishing. Likeable girls are generally kind, assertive and help others, rather than trying to dominate. They are less likely to develop addictions, depression and anxiety, and more likely to create mutually satisfying relationships with friends and partners who will better enjoy spending time with them. Likeability has tremendous implications for the way girls relate to others and their success in many areas of life.

Miswantings describes wanting something that will not be as beneficial as thought. Miswantings can change girls' developmental trajectories. While girls may tend to want status popularity during adolescence, status popularity is mismatched with what is best for their wellbeing and future success. Status popularity can be costly as it provides a distraction and missteps away from relatedness and flourishing. The next chapter explores miswantings that may become a source of excessive competition between peers to 'climb higher on the stairs'. These miswantings can involve an extrinsic focus on grades, future wealth, excessive admiration and fame.

SUMMARY OF KEY POINTS

- Deconstruct the term popularity with your daughter.

- Talk about the risks and costs of using prosocial and coercive behaviours to obtain status popularity and social dominance.

- Highlight the numerous long-term benefits from likeable popularity and authentic connections with peers.

Miswantings

Beware what you set your heart upon. For it surely shall be yours.

- RALPH WALDO EMERSON

Miswanting is a word used by psychologists Tim Wilson and Daniel Gilbert, to refer to wanting something that is not as good for us as we think it will be, and that will not make us as happy as we believe it will. It describes the mismatch between how we are evaluating our life, and our wellbeing and happiness. Status popularity involves building oneself up to be more than others and competing with others for status markings. Whilst it is normal for our daughters to have a desire for status, the excessive pursuit of high status will be unlikely to foster wellbeing.

Why do we have miswantings? Towards the end of my studies, I worked casually leading tutorial groups for undergraduate students. One of these tutorials involved hypotheses testing the Muller-Lyer illusion. In this illusion, a line with the inward pointing arrows looks significantly longer than the other line with the outward pointing arrows, although it is not.

This illusion outlines how there can be a disconnect between our perceptions and reality. The perception of the image given to the brain is faulty. It is this faulty perception that leads to miswantings. Laurie Santos, a professor of psychology from Yale University and teacher of the Science of Well-Being course, outlines how our intuitions about what will be good for us are not always accurate due to 'annoying features of the brain'. Firstly, we tend to think in relative terms and use comparison reference points that are often unrealistic rather than thinking in absolutes. We also get used to things we obtain, changing what is expected over time, referred to as hedonic adaptation. Things you obtain may seem tremendous or terrible at first, but, eventually, you get used to them. Consequently, your reference point is also reset for future judgements. In terms of having little insight, we do not consider hedonic adaptation and overestimate the impact and length of time of the emotional effect. We do not tend to get better at recognising this bias over time.

EXTRINSIC VERSES INTRINSIC GOALS

Motivations for status trappings are mostly extrinsic rather than intrinsic, and this influences happiness and wellbeing. Self-determination theory outlines the importance of pursuing intrinsically motivated goals, which are described as being motivated by the self. They are interesting, enjoyable and are expressive of inherent growth. In contrast, extrinsic goals are experienced as externally controlled and are pursued for an outcome not linked directly to basic psychological needs.

There are three basic psychological needs: autonomy, competence and relatedness. Autonomy is feeling that your actions are self-endorsed, voluntary and based on your values or interests. Competence refers to feeling effective and capable in your undertakings and extending abilities. Relatedness is feeling authentically connected with and belonging to, giving and receiving from others.

A girl's psychological needs can be compared to the three requirements of a plant to grow and thrive. A plant cannot grow properly without the right amount of water, sun and nutrients in the soil. Likewise, girls cannot grow properly without the right amount of autonomy, competence and relatedness. When these three needs are not prioritised, a girl's psychological health suffers. Our girls' goals, therefore, are greatest when they are linked to psychological needs and intrinsically motivated.

The importance of setting the right goals is highlighted in a study conducted by psychology professor Chris Niemiec and his colleagues from the University of Rochester. Students were asked about their life goals and followed for several years. The study found that students' intentions directed their behaviour over an extended period of time and increased the likelihood of attaining the goals they set. However, not all goals were equally beneficial for social functioning and wellbeing. The attainment of extrinsic goals, such as money, fame and image, was related to poorer wellbeing, including depression, anxiety and physical complaints. Positive wellbeing was linked to intrinsic goal achievements, such as the attainment of personal growth, close relationships and physical health. Changes in youths' psychological health were mediated by changes in their attainment of autonomy, competence and relatedness.

Western society has undergone significant generational changes during the last five decades, with an increasing focus on extrinsic goals. A study by psychologist Jean Twenge and her colleagues found that high school students in recent times tend to endorse more extrinsic goals, such as goals for money, fame and image, compared to past generations. These life goals seem to have overtaken the importance of intrinsic goals such as self-acceptance, affiliation and community. Concern for others also declined over time, including empathy for those not within the individual's social group and working in jobs assisting others. The problem is that extrinsic motivations have the power to undermine intrinsic motivation.

GRADES AND FUTURE CAREER

When there is an excessive focus on image and admiration, girls may choose goals, such as good grades and a high earning career, to support their pursuit of status. However, focusing on the grade as the outcome will steal from the deep motivation girls inherently have for learning due to the change from intrinsic to extrinsic orientation. The more obsessed a girl becomes about grades, the more it strips away her love of learning, having a counterintuitive and potentially counterproductive effect on her learning process. This is not to say that a girl will not work hard if she is extrinsically motivated, but her motivation to work will be missing as soon as the rewards are absent.

Another problem with an excessive focus on grades is that it takes a girl away from a *growth* mindset and towards a *fixed* mindset. Carol Dweck, a leading researcher and advocate of growth mindsets, describes two different ways of thinking about intelligence. When one has a fixed mindset, there is the belief that intelligence is innate and fixed. Therefore, outcomes reveal one's intelligence or lack thereof. Consequently, a girl with a fixed mindset links grades to self-worth and status and may be more likely to cheat for better grades or go to great lengths to conceal or avoid deficiencies. Grades become about competition rather than learning. In contrast, a growth mindset results in persistence, and outcomes provide feedback to help growth.

A study by neuroscience researchers Jennifer Mangels and colleagues from the City University of New York provides support for a neurocognitive model for the mechanism underlying differences in fixed and growth mindsets and performance. Those students who endorsed performance goals, including, 'When I take a course in school, it is very important for me to validate that I am smarter than other students,' had more significant attention signals in response to negative feedback, implying that this information is very salient or threatening. Students who endorsed a growth mindset and learning goals, including, 'It is very important to me to feel that my coursework offers me real challenges,' showed more attention signals to the correct answers. Feedback changed student brain event-related potentials about test outcomes. So, whilst it may seem beneficial to care about grades, caring about learning is more powerful, leading to learning success over time.

Focusing on a girl's rankings of grades may also facilitate aggression and competition for status.

'What the ... ?' Lilly thought as she looked over at Bella.

Lilly had entered the history class apprehensively as she knew the test results would be back today. Things had been tough for Lilly over the last couple of months since her aunt died, and she was not sure how she had done on the exam.

To Lilly's surprise, when she entered the classroom, she saw Bella waving her exam paper above her head with a massive grin on her face and wiggling her hips.

'Lilly got 60 per cent ... Nah Nah Nah.' Bella put the words into a song.

Bella had positioned herself so that she was blocking Lilly's access to the board at the front of the room, where she had also written Lilly's test result on the chalkboard in large bold numbers for everyone to see.

Fear gripped Lilly, and she instinctively lunged at her paper, yelling, 'Give it back!'

Lilly could feel her muscles tensing and adrenaline pumping through her as she struggled to grab the paper from Bella. Bella's eyes flashed with excitement and confidence that she could hold the paper for a little bit longer despite Lilly's attempts to get it from her.

Lilly eventually grabbed the paper, then wiped her mark off the board and hurried to her desk. She kept her eyes down as soft giggles waffled through the classroom.

'Loser,' said Bella under her breath.

At this moment, the teacher walked into the room. 'Hi girls, I have left your marked papers on my desk for you to collect'.

'Congratulations, Bella, on topping the class,' the teacher exclaimed.

Bella's misguided focus on her grade was a form of psychological needs substitution or collateral satisfaction. The happiness Bella may have expected from getting a good grade is likely overestimated. Studies show that students predict that they will be happier than they are when getting a good grade and not as miserable as they predict after getting a lower-than-expected grade. Despite Bella's song and dance about getting a better grade than Lilly, the reality is that Lilly's test score did not measure her intelligence nor future potential in the subject. Instead, it measured her mastery of the material in the examination at a specific point in time under certain circumstances.

Lilly's teacher was unaware of Bella's cruelty towards Lilly before she entered the classroom. This story highlights how it is not unusual for bistrategic controllers to avoid detection due to their high level of strategic and competent social skills and acceptance by the larger group. Bistrategic resource controllers may routinely engage in helpfulness to teachers and correct and report on peers' behaviours.

So, how can a classroom teacher encourage girls to set intrinsic goals for learning? When a girl feels liked and less controlled by her teacher, she will become more intrinsically motivated to learn. A good relationship with a teacher extends further to many aspects of a girl's wellbeing, not just how well she performs academically but also her emotional health and sense of belonging in the school.

A girl's intrinsic motivation for her studies is probably the single best predictor of her engagement and, therefore, her ultimate achievement. To move your daughter towards intrinsic goals for her studies, encourage her to be curious, to enjoy learning for the sake of learning and to embrace challenges. A girl with a growth mindset will place a higher value on education, seek out work and process learning more deeply. Grades become helpful for feedback on learning and growth, including which areas might require more work. We need to celebrate our daughters' efforts and hard work.

We can support our daughters to set the right learning goals by talking with them about their plans and *why* these goals are important. Our daughters will flourish when they focus on doing the best they can, not trying to *be* the best.

At this point, you may be feeling confused and thinking that your daughter needs to focus on good grades so she can get a good job when she finishes school. However, Santos outlines how some work goals are also miswantings. Focusing on getting a high-status job that earns a lot of money is, at best, only indirectly related to your daughter's basic psychological needs. Choosing a career for a higher income will only make a girl happy if she lives at very low-income levels. Once a girl's basic needs are met, earning extra income will not increase her wellbeing and overall happiness. In fact, the pursuit of money may hinder or interfere with her psychological needs.

The more importance is placed on goals to obtain wealth, the more symptoms of ill-being and unhappiness people experience.

Even when attaining financial goals, there is a decrease in a person's happiness and vitality. Furthermore, being paid more money in a job results in beliefs that to be happy, one needs to earn even more money again. However, there seems to be limited insight to this, as when asked, people believe that they must be happier because they earn a large amount of money, even when they are not.

So, perhaps we need to reconsider the criteria for career success and, in doing so, reduce the pressure on our girls to meet specific markers. A good job is one that allows our daughters to use their strengths and follow their inclinations to create meaning. Strengths vary between each of us, and so engaging with our own unique strengths in a career results in flourishing and happiness. The more that young women can use their strengths in the workplace, the more positive and productive they will become, and the higher they will rate their job satisfaction.

FAME

Since our culture values and celebrates fame, why wouldn't our girls want this also? Approximately one-third of the population is estimated to be affected by celebrity worship syndrome. Celebrities are, in a way, the popular kids of the adult world. Their popularity is visible on social media and influences other's attitudes and buying patterns. However, the outcome of fame is not all it seems. In a study involving interviews with 15 celebrities, including representatives from various societal roles such as a politician, a film actor, TV personalities, a highly ranked CEO, sports athletes, a celebrity lawyer, a musician and a child actor, researchers Donna Rockwell and David Giles found that there are some common patterns among them in their experience of fame.

At first, the celebrities found the admiration and special treatment pleasurable in a kind of addictive way. Hypervigilance emerged to keep and even increase the accolades. However, others' opinions of them were out of their control. Extrinsic motivation for positive feedback from others often led to heightened self-consciousness about selling an image and holding back on their authentic self.

Next, the losses to personal freedoms in everyday routine and privacy prevented the celebrities from enjoying little pleasures in life. New behaviours emerged, such as pretending not to see or hear others in public and becoming more reclusive. Celebrity status damaged their relationships, as mistrust grew about the motivations of people's interest in them. They were concerned that some people wanted to take advantage of their celebrity status for either money or increases in their status, and they found that many people liked them but didn't know them on a deeper personal level nor care about them. Alienation and loneliness increased.

Over time, anxiety about the impact of fame on family members and other close, pre-fame relationships emerged. These close relationships suffered as loved ones felt inferior to and disconnected from the celebrity. Furthermore, the demands of celebrity life also reduced time with their loved ones and increased the presence of other distractions that moved them away from treating their family well. Celebrities started to feel emotionally isolated from their loved ones.

In the end, there seemed to be a tendency for those having fame to wish for something else. And that something else involved finding meaning, connection and authenticity. People wanted to get back to who they really are. So, whilst it is normal for your daughter to strive for status, excessive status pursuits will unlikely lead to her wellbeing and thriving. Encourage her to seek the middle road. Mindfulness is a tool that can help with miswantings by opening a space between urges and behaviours. The more mindful girls become, the more likely it is that they will respond to cravings compassionately and wisely.

SUMMARY OF KEY POINTS

- Support your daughter to pursue intrinsic goals for her studies and future career.

- Emphasise pursuits based on her values and interests, help her feel capable in extending her abilities, and provide opportunities for relatedness rather than comparisons.

Unpacking Gossip

Any fool can know. The point is to understand.
– ALBERT EINSTEIN

One of the main reasons girls engage in relational aggression is to increase or maintain their social status and power. Relational aggression often successfully promotes a girl and her group as socially superior. It can feel good to be positively distinguished from others. During adolescence, girls' social sophistication and relational aggression, including the tool of gossip, increase.

THE GOSSIP PARADOX

When we unpack gossip, its paradoxical nature is exposed. Gossip refers to speaking about another person or persons when they are not present, and often involves some form of evaluative comments about a person's behaviour. We all talk about other people at times. However, while gossip can be damaging, especially when used as a tool for relational aggression, it can also be neutral or positive.

Sharing information and experiences that are yours to share can facilitate connection and support in friendships, which is on the right path to likeability. Should your daughter know something about another person's behaviour that protects another girl, not providing that information might even be considered wrong. Gossip can be prosocial.

Many of the girls I meet with talk to me about others when they are not present. Girls want to find helpful ways to manage social dilemmas and respond to tricky situations with people they know. Talking can help a girl process a relationship by facilitating increased insight, allowing her to respond more thoughtfully. It also affords her opportunities to regulate her emotions.

The dark side of gossip is the use of information about a girl to degrade and exclude her. It often involves sharing information that is not the gossipers to share. Using gossip to mistreat another girl is a psychologically sophisticated way of harming another person whilst denying intent to hurt, thereby avoiding detection. As with other forms of relational aggression, when gossiping in a socially competent manner, the status of the gossiper increases.

Research shows that status popular peers gossip more than less popular peers. Status popular girls have higher self-esteem, are more socially central and are more successful at convincingly spreading information. The topic of gossip usually involves peer relationships, general behaviours and characteristics, associations, physical attractiveness, fashion and sexual behaviours.

Gossip provides four main functions:

- It sets the norms for the group for what or who is okay or not
- It boosts the social standing of the members perpetrating gossip

- It provides a fun and entertaining way of strengthening relationships within the group
- It has the power to manipulate the group's feelings about a person.

Lilly's story is an excellent illustration of how this works.

'Here, Lilly, have a drink.'

Ben passed Lilly a can of beer. Lilly confidently took a mouthful and handed it back.

Lilly was wearing her favourite jeans and a white jumper with black stripes. She had put a lot of thought and effort into her outfit for the party. She didn't want to come across as 'trying too hard' by wearing her best clothes, so she purposely chose a casual outfit.

Lilly could feel the energy in the room and was thrilled to be a part of it. She was eager to be there because she wanted to reconnect with Sophia. Sophia had been her best friend since starting high school. She had studied with her, shared secrets about boys she liked, had fun at sleepovers watching movies and eating junk food and consulted her on all sorts of problems, including what course she would do after leaving school. Recently, Sophia was hanging more around the popular group and less around Lilly.

As the night went on, everyone was drinking, talking and laughing. Sophia had too much to drink and vomited. Lilly stood by her, holding her hair back from her face. Bella, in the popular group, was not too impressed that

Lilly was at the party for a start, but even more annoyed at seeing her getting on so well with everyone.

At the end of the night, Ben pulled out a joint and passed it around. Lilly took a puff along with several of the other boys in the group.

The next day at school, stories about the weekend party circulated. With her face wrinkled in disgust, Bella told the girls in her group that Lilly is a 'druggo'. Bella also told her mother that Lilly used drugs and for this reason, she and Sophia did not hang around Lilly. Bella's mother was concerned about the drug use and agreed that Lilly should not be invited to the next party. Bella's mother also warned her friends who had children at the same school about Lilly's behaviour.

Bella's reputational damage to Lilly came under the disguise of protecting the peer group from drug-taking risks. The gossip did not accurately report the night's events as it excluded information about other peers' drug use and exaggerated Lilly's involvement. By manipulating the information, Bella elevated her status with adults by portraying herself as a desirable, responsible adolescent and she was able to keep the parties for exclusive peers only.

I first met Lilly in the waiting room of my private practice. She had long brown hair and a slender build. Her smile, although broad and polite, was not accompanied by happiness in her eyes. She followed me to my office, looked around and sat down. She avoided eye contact as she told me a familiar story. Lilly's friends had stopped sitting with her at lunch, she was not invited to parties and her classmates' parents, with whom she previously had a good relationship, had been much less friendly towards her. She now went straight to the senior study rooms at school where she worked alone during lunch breaks.

When the peer group changes their perception of a girl or receives an advantage from gossip through social comparison, it is difficult for girls to assess the context honestly. The gossip increased Bella's closeness with the girls she gave preferential treatment to, whilst her willingness to mistreat Lilly showed her strength to prevent disloyalty from other group members. Don't assume that just because many girls are spreading the same gossip that they or you know what is going on. It is common for girls to accept girls who mistreat others. They are also most likely willing to participate or be quiet to ensure that they do not receive the same treatment.

As in Lilly's story, gossip may involve dishonesty and at the root of this is the presence of two opposing motives: honesty and advantage. Dishonesty increases during adolescence compared to childhood, perhaps due to an increasing desire for autonomy. However, adolescence is also a crucial period in the development of moral action and justice beliefs. Lying can be considered risk-taking behaviour because the more a person lies, the more likely they will lie in the future. Brain scans show changing neural mechanisms following lying, which support this proposition. The more we lie, the fewer emotional responses become evoked prompting us to put a brake on deceit. Effectively, people start to become desensitised. Small acts of dishonesty are gateway behaviours that can lead to more significant acts of dishonesty.

When making sense of gossip, consider the context, motivation and possible functions behind it. It is vital to step back and assess both *what* is being said and *why* it is being said.

DRUGS

Brain changes in the adolescent years lead to novelty seeking and creative exploration. Adolescents have an increased inner motivation to try new things coupled with a sense of adventure. The downside is that, at times, the thrill of sensation seeking and risk-taking is overemphasised, whilst the potentially harmful consequences are minimised. It is not what parents like to hear, but girls will be exposed to drugs at parties. Alcohol, cigarettes, cannabis and other illegal drug use increases in frequency during adolescence. From a survey of 20,000 secondary school students in 2017, 85 per cent of youth have consumed alcohol by the age of 17 years, and 17 per cent have used illicit drugs (e.g. heroin and cannabis).

There are good reasons to guide girls away from drug use. At parties, drugs impair judgement in a situation where a girl needs to make good decisions, especially to keep herself and her friends safe. In addition, adolescent drug use is associated with lower academic performance, increased physical and mental health problems, unhealthy peer relations and injury.

Drug use in adolescence is a multifactorial problem. At a time when peers matter a lot, the quality of a youth's friendships plays a role in substance use. Loneliness is linked to increased alcohol consumption and positive relationships may have a protective effect. Ironically, Lilly's mistreatment by her peers may have increased her future drug use. Likewise, using substances to impress certain peers or develop a sense of belonging may also increase a girl's use. Girls who are supervised, feel connected with their family, are happy in themselves and believe they are achieving are less likely to use drugs. When hearing gossip about peer drug use, focus on caring about peers instead of judging a person's character.

From a practical viewpoint, help your daughter make plans for minimising problems with drugs. Firstly, talking to her about drug use, rather than avoiding the topic, will help her be honest with you. Secondly, focus on conversations about her mental and physical health and her and her classmates' safety at a party. Make drugs the problem, not peers. Recognising that parties represent a highly tricky situation for drug use, she can problem-solve steps to manage this effectively. Perhaps she could have a stash of non-alcoholic drinks in small bottles at home to grab on her way out the door. The plan might involve helping her to say 'no thanks'. If she does not feel strong enough to be assertive with peers pressuring her to use drugs, you might have an agreement where she can text you a code word and then you will phone her, telling her that you urgently need her home despite her protests in front of any observers. Most importantly, have a rule where she will never get into trouble for phoning you to pick her up, whatever the circumstances, without questions.

BOYS

Friendships with boys can be equally as kind and supportive as friendships with girls. One of my daughters shared with me that her friendships with boys during senior school were essential sources of fun and inclusion. Many of these friendships have endured and the boys have grown into trustworthy, honest, caring young men.

Relationships may grow into more intimate romantic connections and this is mostly positive. With approximately 60 per cent of grade 12 students engaging in sex, the focus is best placed on health and respect. The emphasis should be on ensuring girls have an equal role in negotiating sexual acts in relationships with other youth. Relationships are about consent, reciprocity, care and connection. If a girl wants something different from her partner, the partner who wants the least of the two needs to be respected.

Emergent sexuality is intertwined with relational aggression in adolescence. A primary motive for girls' aggression is to enhance their sexual status and access to desired boys. Getting along with boys, particularly desirable boys, can increase a girl's status and, therefore, the likelihood of being targeted by gossip and name-calling by competing girls. By spreading gossip, a girl can reduce another girl's sexual appeal and access to boys. Unfortunately, boys' aggression may also take on a sexual nature.

To better understand relational aggression in adolescence, it is crucial to understand that boys also engage in relational aggression. Boys will gossip about girls for the same reasons as girls, such as to obtain status increases and inclusion in otherwise exclusionary groups. An estimated 80 to 90 per cent of adolescent girls have experienced sexual harassment, including LGBTQI+ girls. Sexual harassment is not about friendship or mutual attraction; it is about power and involves uninvited sexual behaviour that is humiliating or intimidating.

SEXTING

The incidence of sending sexual images, or sexting, varies in adolescence from an estimated 6 to 49 per cent of girls and 15 to 32 per cent of boys. There are many stories, such as Laura's story, where sexual images have been misused to gain status.

> Laura sat perched on the edge of a chair in my office. She eyed me cautiously. We were meeting after her GP had referred her for anxiety. After I introduced myself, I explained what I understood about her reasons for attending.
>
> 'Your GP says that at times you are experiencing trouble breathing and shake a lot.'
>
> Laura nodded.
>
> 'Can you tell me more about what is going on for you?' I asked. Laura explained that she had recently finished high school and had started her first year at college. However, she found it difficult to complete her first university practicum due to fears about making mistakes and being afraid that her colleagues thought poorly of her.
>
> Within a couple more meetings, Laura was able to challenge anxiety-provoking thoughts, including self-critical thoughts. She was also able to be mindful of body sensations that accompanied anxiety and better slow her breathing to calm herself.
>
> Laura also started unfolding the history of put-downs from her father, which resulted in her turning to her peers for belonging in high school. Unfortunately, her attempts to connect with peers were met with social cruelty.

Laura explained the series of events. 'The girls didn't like me. Mandy made fun of what I wore, and one day, when a teacher was late for math class, a group of girls were talking about me and laughing. My heart was racing, and all I could think of was that I needed to escape.'

'That's tough,' I empathised.

Laura continued. 'A couple of days later, I was so excited when Tom approached me to go on a date to the movies. The date went well, and afterwards, he messaged asking for a nude photograph.' She paused, clearly embarrassed. 'I didn't want to, but when I said no, Tom got angry at me. He said that if I could not do this, I didn't like him enough to be his girlfriend. I was so afraid of losing him, and I had heard the other girls at school talk about doing that sort of stuff with their boyfriends, so I eventually agreed.'

The story ended with Tom sharing the photograph with his friends and never speaking to Laura again. The girls ostracised Laura further, now calling her derogatory names.

'I have been too ashamed to tell anyone before,' Laura disclosed as she looked at the floor through a steady stream of tears. Laura had been carrying this secret for the past couple of years. She worried that the photograph might still be circulating and re-emerge to humiliate her again in future.

My heart went out to Laura. Her wanting closeness, support and affection resulted in an impulsive decision to send a photo, with the outcome being further isolation and cruelty. Tom, on the other hand, had increased his social status with his peers. It is noteworthy that often gossip about sex and drugs focuses on the girl. It can be a good idea to ask your daughter to consider whether the boys involved are being talked about in the same way.

Sexting may be increasingly normalised, but it does have the potential to abuse through control and humiliation. Girls seem to bear the brunt of this. A girl will be criticised if she sends the photo, but condemned if she does not. Sending a sexually explicit photo can please another person and create a sense of inclusion and belonging, and it can also alleviate repeated harassment or anger towards a girl. Girls often feel at the mercy of a series of social and relational pressures they are anxious about handling.

While impulsivity and risk-taking have always increased in adolescence, prior generations had more privacy when making reactive or poor decisions. Girls are criticised for sending images due to the possibility of unintended audiences, mass distribution, emotional distress and adverse parental reactions. With rapid technological changes, our girls are dealing with genuine concerns about the dissemination of their private information, which may or may not be associated with legal implications related to storing or transmitting sexual images of a minor.

The sexual landscape has also changed for our girls. The rapid access to technology has coincided with the rise of pornography and changing young people's attitudes and behaviours around sex. Sexting may be conceptualised as a process whereby young people produce their own pornography. Up to 80 to 99 per cent of young people are estimated to have viewed sexually explicit material, boys more so than girls, citing educational and entertainment purposes.

The increase in pornography is problematic for several reasons. Sexually explicit images typically share the similarities of objectifying and sexualising females. In pornography, obtaining sexual pleasure is more important than emotional attachment and caring about another person. The message our girls need to hear is that pornography does not reflect real sex or relationships. Furthermore, the imagery tends to perpetuate normative views in our culture that males dominate sexual situations and is linked to risk-taking and coercion. Ensure your daughter knows it is not okay for a person to ask her for sexual photos or continue asking after being told no.

A student's petition detailing thousands of alleged sexual assaults against female students recently highlighted the extent of the problem of sexual coercion and violence in our high schools. Girls have disclosed being forced to perform sexual acts at parties and being inappropriately touched. In response, the government has improved school students' education about respectful relationships, consent and sexual abuse. As a result, there is increasing public awareness of the prevalence of the coercive control of females, which is not exclusively occurring in schools or with adolescent girls.

Gently talk about and model healthy intimate relationships and contrast this with controlling and dominating relationships. Remind your daughter that it is illegal for anyone to engage with her in sexual activity without her full consent. The tea analogy is applicable here: you do not make someone drink a cup of tea if they don't want to or are unconscious. Having a cup of tea once doesn't mean they want a cup of tea again. If someone wants tea, then changes their mind, they don't have to drink the tea. It is not okay to pour tea down someone's throat when they don't want tea, and it's the same with sex.

We can teach our daughters to challenge society's norms that create inequality for girls. What is typical for females, and who decided this? Many years ago, when my three daughters were young, my sister Henia bought them a book by Babette Cole titled *Princess Smarty Pants*. The book tells the story of a pretty and rich princess who lives in a castle and who everyone expects to marry a handsome prince. The problem is that Princess Smarty Pants loves animals, adventures in the wild and getting messy. She is not interested in getting married, and with ingenuity and grit, she overcomes obstacles to create the life that she wants. As Henia was reading the book to the girls, one of my daughters asked. 'Why was the princess called Smarty Pants?' Henia smiled. 'Because despite being frowned on by the people around her for not doing what they wanted, she was smart enough to follow her own path.'

SUMMARY OF KEY POINTS

- Gossip about peer drug use and sexual activity provides excellent opportunities to talk kindly and gently with our daughters about the realities of adolescence.

- Guide them to prioritise their mental and physical health and think critically about society's norms for women.

- Crucially, an episode of gossip is an opportunity to practise inclusive and respectful behaviours towards others by modelling to our girls that we don't share information that is not ours to share.

Exclusion Strategies

If a circle shuts you out, draw a circle around it.
– MARTY RUBIN

Relational aggression involves efforts to exclude a girl from her social group. Exclusion is the process of acting to prevent or block someone from taking part in an activity or entering a setting. It is the act of purposefully not considering or including someone. The function of exclusion is often to create a special and elite group (the included) and control social rewards.

I found myself relying heavily on supportive strategies in the context of exclusion when following up with Lilly. It had been several weeks since Lilly had learned that Bella had spread the rumour that she was a 'druggo' and she had been getting the cold shoulder from her classmates. Bella and Sophia and their group kept having parties on weekends and posting photos of the parties on social media.

'All the friends I had from the first party, including Nick and Ben, were there. I can tell they are having fun from the Instagram photos. I saw Nick sitting on Sophia's lap.' Lilly looked crushed. 'The girls all had new leather boots, which I have wanted now for a while, but Mum said I couldn't have them because they are too expensive,' explained Lilly.

'On Friday night, I was okay, enjoying watching movies on my own, until heaps of photos of the latest party came through on social media. I don't care what they do anymore, but why do I have to see it?' I could tell from the way that Lilly spoke that she was hurting.

I knew that Lilly would most likely protest at the suggestion that she go without social media for a while.

'Even though I didn't want to, I stayed up late looking at the party to see who was there. All the girls in my grade were posting comments about how wonderful Bella and Sophia are. I just felt sick and couldn't sleep.'

The online show of social support resulted in Lilly feeling bad about herself for not being included.

SOCIAL MEDIA

The rapid increase in the widespread use of technology by young people can exacerbate a girl's feelings of being left out. Not being included is hurtful, but it is even more painful to see it advertised on social media. There is no denying that social media has changed our daughters' social interactions. The impact has been dramatic, with most teens connected online at an estimated seven to nine hours per day. TV, movies, computers, mobile games and iPhones permeate a girl's life over time and across settings.

Girls focused on status popularity in face-to-face peer interactions are most likely doing the same on social media. The platform allows for pictures and videos signalling physical attractiveness, fashion and affiliations. The number of *friends* and *likes* or comments a girl receives is a measurable reflection of her social networks and the strength of her affiliations. Girls interact with other girls online, leaving positive comments and liking their friends' posts, thereby boosting each other's social media presence and status. It is the perfect format to create a desirable social identity as visible, admired and influential. However, their creation of positive emotional links with selective others, is always to the exclusion of some, and girls who are not part of this can be left palpably aware of it.

Studies show that when a youth sees that something is liked by the group on social media, they will like it more. The impact of cravings for social media likes and following the things peers like are seen in brain scans that show greater neural activation in areas implicated in attention, social cognition, reward processing and imitation. Youth are more likely to *like* photos they think peers have liked and *not like* photos they think peers have not liked, even when a computer program artificially generates these likes. Girls' preferences and behaviours are manipulated by perceived popularity online, and the girls have little insight into the manipulation.

We have known for a while that companies are becoming wealthy by targeting girls' buying behaviours. The fashion and body product industry spend billions annually on marketing, often using celebrities. Leveraging celebrity status or modern popularity communicates emotionally evocative messages and influences adolescent thoughts. The media serves as a viral *super peer*, creating opportunities for shaping adolescent social normative beliefs beyond direct peer contact. The industry encourages excessive consumerism and suggests that girls need to improve their appearance, including promoting sexualisation and thinness. Status popular girls tend to be the most likely to conform to social media norms, including media promoted appearance, behaviours and other attributes. A girl is told if she looks the right way, has the right clothes and owns the right material possessions, she will be happier. Media, such as reality TV shows and drama series, also play a role in relational aggression. Studies have found that the more these shows are watched, the more likely a girl will behave aggressively with her peers. Media can give girls the message that it is normal to be aggressive to *get* more and *buy* more, to *be* more.

Social media upward comparisons occur when girls compare themselves to other girls with perceived superior characteristics and can considerably reduce a girl's self-esteem. When girls see other girls online looking prettier, more stylish and socialising more, it impacts. Humans are sensitive to context and where we stand relative to other people. Our minds tend to pick faulty reference points, resulting in a distorted perception, much like the effect of the Ebbinghaus visual illusion. In this illusion, circles around the centre circle make the centre circles appear different from each other. Both centre circles are the same size, but we do not accurately see this because of the reference point of the outside circles. Similarly, girls tend to judge themselves relative to reference points on social media that are often irrelevant.

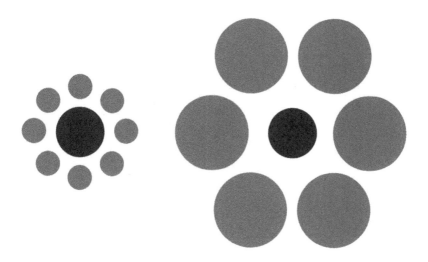

Researchers say that we may have underestimated the harm to girls from the internet and social media. A recent study of over 11,000 adolescents by Jean Twenge and colleagues found that girls who are on the internet five hours per day or more were 166 per cent more likely to be experiencing significant depressive symptoms than girls who were low users of the internet. Girls were more negatively affected by screen media time than boys. The more a girl spends time on screen media, the poorer her mental health and wellbeing. We can find ways of managing media with our daughters. Perhaps computers can be kept in a shared space at home, a cut off time agreed on for computer and phone use at night and computer-free family time scheduled.

Whilst there is little harm in having pride in your appearance or being creative and having fun playing around with hair and makeup, a girl's appearance is one of her most superficial qualities. Whenever you can, draw attention away from how a girl looks to focus on her body's health. Downplay outward looks and raise the importance of qualities and strengths she can cultivate. Encourage your daughter to befriend and nurture her body. Encourage her to eat nutritious food, with junk food being 'sometimes' food. Encourage her to engage in team exercises focusing on building her strengths and skill. Model these principles and do healthy activities together as a family. Help her develop scepticism about how media represents females.

We can challenge our daughter's comparison of her real self with the online idealised self of others. Social networking sites are not an accurate reflection of people or their lives, as it is not portraying the actual person, with all their unique complexities and human layers. Instead, it is a series of preferred and tailored images. The reality is that online friends are not always people who know much about the substance of other online friends. So, a girl is not getting an accurate representation of other people. Girls also do not get the proper distribution of events occurring in someone else's life – the content posted online tends to be a curated, edited highlight reel. Challenge girls to think about online postings from another perspective.

'Why was that picture or video posted?'

'Who was that picture posted for?'

'What is the message for viewers of this photo?'

In moving our daughters towards likeability, encourage the use of social media to give to others rather than elevate oneself. Girls can use the online world to be kind to others, share helpful information and authentically connect. Messenger groups and online forums can provide a way for girls to find belonging. This can increase a girl's friendship base, social and emotional support, perspective-taking and sense of worthiness.

Lilly and I continued meeting after she had disclosed that she was spending every lunch break at school in a small study room on her own. The school's senior study area had a common room with a small kitchenette and lounges to make drinks and snacks during study breaks. Branching off from the common room was a series of small study offices which fit several desks and had enough room for two or three students. The design of the small study rooms was to help the girls focus on study without distractions; however, Lilly had been using the seclusion of the rooms to withdraw during lunch.

'There is no point,' Lilly confided. 'If I go out into the common room or the outside courtyard, no-one includes me anyway. Everyone already has a best friend or group of friends. I get along well with Mia, but her best friend Mandy gives me bad looks if I sit near her at lunch. It's not worth the effort.'

'I'm sorry to hear that,' I gently commented.

Lilly looked at the ground and then back at me before replying angrily, 'Yeah, it is crap'. Underneath the anger, I sensed a deep sadness.

I focused on helping Lilly make room for her emotional storm with self-compassion. It was important for Lilly to direct care and concern towards her suffering and accept her pain in a kind way.

'At least Mandy only gives me bad looks when I sit with Mia. If I go near a girl who is even kind of popular, Bella runs over, grabs her and pulls her away from me. Bella is so nice to everyone but me. People now look uncomfortable when I go near them. It's sort of like they'll be in trouble if they talk to me. I don't know why Bella has to watch me and make sure that no-one else will be my friend. She has lots of friends. I wish she would just leave me alone.'

I reflected a moment. 'It doesn't sound like Bella is ready to change or that the girls in your grade are prepared to go against Bella.'

'How do you feel about going over the things that are in your control?' I tentatively queried.

Lilly reluctantly nodded in agreement.

At least she seemed like she would hear me out. Together Lilly and I came up with a list of things that she likes to do, such as walking her dog, painting, dancing to music, drinking hot chocolate, watching a movie with her sister and so on. She agreed to make sure that she did one of these things every day. Next, she made a list of people she likes and who treat her well. This list included her history teacher, her mum and an aunt. She agreed to talk with them regularly. Although adults and family can positively impact a girl's relatedness, I knew Lilly needed friendships with peers. Having at least one or two friends is incredibly protective for a girl. Girls have a lot to lose when they lose friends.

'Is there anyone that you know out of school that you could spend time with?' I questioned. It is always a good thing to foster opportunities for friendships outside of school.

'Well, I'm not sure they would want to, but there are a couple of girls from my netball team from last year that go to the school across the road. I get along well with them but don't get to see much of them outside of netball. And then there are a couple of boys from a different school I knew even before I went to the party. I got along really well with them, and I know that made Bella angry, but I think that they still want to be friends with me.'

I encouraged her to reach out to other young people and reminded her that she had nothing to lose.

After several weeks, Lilly started to build some new friendships. She had expressed an interest in being friends with a wide range of peers by inviting them to do things with her, being prosocial and positive and not taking it personally when it didn't always work out. Now, she was catching up with girls from her old netball team outside of school occasionally and she was part of a messenger chat with a small group of boys. At school, Lilly focused on being friendly with both Mia and Mandy. The three girls had started to become closer and sat together at lunch. Before school, Lilly would go to Mia's house to make pancakes for breakfast. She was starting to feel better.

Social exclusion is a common experience, as is having challenges in friendships. Many girls need some time and a little support to find ways of reconnecting or making new connections with peers. Some inherent unfairness around exclusion represents the lack of fit between a girl and her group. Fitting in is about becoming who you need to be in a particular group in order to be accepted. Fitting in actually presents a barrier to belonging, as belonging involves being vulnerable enough to be who you are when connecting with others. It takes much more courage to be vulnerable and embrace our imperfections and resist changing who we are, than to fit in.

Our daughters must be proactive about finding connections and belonging, as isolated girls are often overlooked. We can encourage our girls to focus on relationships with people they have had previous positive experiences with and create new opportunities for belonging. If needed, contact the school to help with this also. Having at least one friend will help your daughter develop and refine her social skills, provide emotional support for adolescent stressors and protect her from becoming a target of bullying.

It may also be helpful to observe if your daughter is doing anything that might be preventing her from showing her peers her great qualities. For example, some girls might withdraw due to anxiety, which can be mistaken for being unfriendly. Should you become aware of anxious or depressive symptoms, which could be a barrier to your daughter having friends, it could be helpful for her to speak to a clinical psychologist.

SCHOOL SYSTEM

Exclusion is, in part, a status hierarchy or power problem within a social system. Peer exclusion and other forms of relational aggression are more common in school systems that normalise status hierarchies. Norms promoting status hierarchies result in higher peer rejection rates, lower academic performance and students experiencing fewer positive feelings about school. All students who observe exclusion and other forms of aggressive peer behaviour in a school system are harmed, not just the targeted girl. When the system normalises the elevation of some people, students stop having emotional reactions to inequality and may develop distorted thinking patterns degrading vulnerable people. Observing social cruelty can change developmental trajectories, making it more likely that affected peers will justify mistreating others in the future.

Does the school have exclusive cliques of students? Studies show that classrooms vary in the extent to which there is within-class variation in individual status. The number and strength of bistrategic controllers strongly influence the extent of the classroom hierarchy. The higher the percentage of bistrategic controllers within a classroom, the stronger the status popularity hierarchy.

Classroom hierarchies can be observed by how peers interact and may be evident in the classroom layout. Lilly explained how the socially dominant girls quickly established a fixed seating plan in her grade 10 English class at the beginning of the year. Lilly described four rows of tables, with chairs placed around each table.

The status popular girls sat on one side of the room with a territorial display of arms splayed across the backs of their chairs or leaning back with their hands interlaced behind their heads, with notebooks and bags spread over the tables.

The remaining girls sat huddled, not taking up much space, around tables at the other side of the room. When Lilly sat too close to the wrong side of the classroom, Bella quickly enforced the hierarchy division.

'Oh wow ... really?!' Bella's eyebrows raised as she glared at Lilly and then turned to her group laughing.

The school climate changes the social context. Taking a more expansive view of the school, consider whether the school endorses status values or goals. A school can minimise or be blind to imbalances of and misuse of power. The school may covertly reinforce some staff and students by supporting false hierarchies of power associated with groups. Does the school value some students who achieve status goals whilst neglecting others? For example, a school may favour youth who achieve good grades or play a particular sport. I was reminded of this when listening to an end-of-year address at an exclusive private girls' school.

'We will miss Kayla and her amazing fashion, Rhianna throwing her netball around the court, Lana winning the athletics competitions, Maggie playing the violin and Emma swimming with speed,' the Head Prefect exclaimed. She was impeccably presented, enthusiastic and well-spoken.

She concluded the valedictory address for the graduating year with an erect posture, subtle smile and backward tilt of her head. 'With the foundation of our schooling, you will not see any of us working in Coles.'

The audience gave a standing ovation as the Head Prefect left the podium and returned to her seat.

The girls singled out for mention in the speech were the Head Girl's clique members, the visible and socially central girls from the unspoken upper echelon of the status hierarchy. These girls were competitive in many areas of their lives.

The mention of working in Coles was the second time that month I had heard derogatory references directed at people who work in supermarkets. The first time was from a grade eight student, Felicity, who had found it challenging to go to school because of anxiety. Felicity's problems with school refusal had started not long after she had moved to town and experienced significant changes in her social group. Together, we worked on anxiety management techniques to return to school in a staged manner with support mechanisms in place.

Felicity had started meeting with her teachers to catch up on missed schoolwork. Many teachers had also taken on a supportive role, providing her with encouragement and advice. Felicity recounted a part of a conversation she had with a well-meaning teacher.

'Mrs McRae told me that if I didn't just get myself in the car in the morning, I would end up working in a supermarket'. The judgement and innuendo increased Felicity's anxiety and reduced her trust in Mrs McRae.

Parents can and should challenge the mindset that some people feel entitled and superior towards others. There is a difference between encouraging girls to strive for their achievements and endorsing comparisons with others they consider inferior. Parents and school environments have the influence to push girls away from judging others and instead focus on their own self-improvement. These notions are consistent with the framework of social pedagogy incorporating the humanistic values of respect for self and the diversity of others. Education systems provide an essential vehicle for promoting social justice by challenging the status quo and having unconditional regard for human dignity.

Every girl should be encouraged to do some hard work in a poorly paid job. To do so is to learn the fundamental link between work and income, to develop a sense of connection to those who perform tasks that benefit others for little personal pay, to learn humility in service to others, and to develop respect for the dignity of those who complete physically demanding tasks. Being born into privilege and having opportunities to build skills is undeserved luck, not a marker of inherent superiority. The supermarket staff are the frontline workers who showed up each day up to work to take care of the rest of us during COVID-19 lockdowns, at significant risk to themselves. We need to recognise the value and contribution of all people.

TEACHERS

Do teachers choose to interact more with some groups of students than others? Does the school executive choose their favoured students for leadership positions rather than follow a fair process of equal opportunity? Do staff behave in socially dominant ways towards some students? Do teachers focus more on teaching or controlling students? Do staff behave in socially dominant ways to other staff? Are rewards systems structured to belittle some people? When the school system is healthy, staff are more likely to engage in healthy ways with each other and students.

A woman I worked with, Jacinta, shared her observations of how a teacher has the power to influence status hierarchies and subsequent relational aggression after she attended a school excursion with her daughter. The excursion involved ten days of hiking. There were two small hiking groups of daughters and mothers, each led by a teacher. Mrs Harrison led one group, and Ms Weber led the other. Jacinta and her daughter were allocated to Ms Weber's group.

Jacinta recounted the events as they unfolded. 'Within a day, many of the louder girls in Ms Weber's group became competitive for Ms Weber's attention, talking to her about fashion and boys and fighting to sit next to her at the front of the bus. Ms Weber joined in laughing, talking loudly and singing with them.

A seating arrangement formed on the bus, separating Ms Weber and the dominant girls from the other girls. Ms Weber shared a tent with a mother whose daughter was in Ms Weber's dominant group of girls. When Jacinta was falling asleep in her tent, which was next to Ms Weber's tent, she overheard Ms Weber and the mother critiquing the girls on the excursion, including her daughter.

'I was shocked,' Jacinta explained. 'How could a teacher gossip with a parent about students?'

Jacinta left her tent and stood at the front of Ms Weber's tent.

'I decided to be assertive,' Jacinta said, and I told Ms Weber, 'I can hear you talking about my daughter'. 'Instead of Ms Weber being embarrassed and apologising, she responded defiantly and exclaimed that she was just talking about all the girls. As if she was entitled and I had the problem for questioning her.'

The next day, Ms Weber ignored Jacinta and her daughter whilst increasing her level of intimacy and fun with the socially dominant group. Each night, Ms Weber called a group meeting to acknowledge one girl for her friendship and present her with a bracelet, which the girl wore until the next ceremony, as a token of appreciation. The bracelet was presented based on preference rather than merit. The ceremony was repeated each night when the chosen girl passed the bracelet to another girl of her choice. The socially dominant group became increasingly competitive in demonstrating extravagant accolades towards others in their group during the passing of the bracelet ceremony.

Night after night, Jacinta watched the non-dominant girls being further marginalised and realised that there were not enough nights left on the hike for the ceremony to include them. Jacinta asked if she could buy a second bracelet to be inclusive to all girls, but Ms Weber refused.

On the last night of camp at dinner, Jacinta sat next to a mother who commented to her that her meal was undercooked. Jacinta replied gently that perhaps she could let the cook know. Jacinta remained seated whilst the mother left. This seat was replaced with one of the socially dominant girls. Jacinta took a bite of her meal and realised she had the same problem as the mother sitting next to her previously. She murmured under her breath that she would have to take her meal back too.

The dominant girl shrivelled her face in disgust at Jacinta and raised her voice. 'I'm sick of you complaining. Why don't you get over yourself!'

'I looked around,' Jacinta recalled, 'and everyone acted as if nothing had happened.'

Jacinta did not report the incident with the student to Ms Weber as she had lost confidence that Ms Weber would deal with the situation fairly. The girl was one of Ms Weber's favoured students.

The most reported reasons students don't inform a teacher about their mistreatment from peers is a lack of closeness with the teacher and lack of trust that the teacher will offer appropriate help. There is generally a lack of understanding that speaking up about cruelty from a more socially dominant girl will likely increase the problem in ways that go undetected by teachers. As Jacinta experienced, being assertive can result in punishment. When power differentials are unacknowledged, complaints can result in a mistreated girl being re-traumatised in closed rooms with the more powerful girl. The result is that the less powerful girl must accept her inequitable position in the social hierarchy as absolute.

The other hiking group, led by Mrs Harrison, did not develop a pronounced status hierarchy and there were no notable incidents of relational aggression. Mrs Harrison paid equal attention to all students, making sure to catch the quieter girls' attention with a nod and smile and occasionally checking in with them. She always maintained professional boundaries around confidentiality. Before the daily bus trip, Mrs Harrison rotated the seating plan, ensuring that all the girls had the opportunity to sit at the front of the bus with the best views. She pinned her group's bracelet to her hiking backpack to represent the strengths and belonging of all girls in her group. The nightly meetings were about communicating with everyone about the next day's schedule.

The girls in Mrs Harrison's group settled nicely, with those girls inclined to be competitive for attention becoming increasingly more cooperative. Whereas the quieter girls gradually grew more assertive and confident to participate. Mrs Harrison's treatment of her students contributed to their increasing autonomy, connectedness and overall flourishing. Teacher inclusion, identity-based sensitivity and kindness all impact a multitude of adolescent developmental outcomes. It is so important to youth that it can even buffer the harmful effects of aggression in the home.

As a parent, be mindful of embedding your daughter in social and educational systems that covertly endorse status hierarchies. Be familiar with the school's code of ethics and expect your daughter and her classmates to be treated with fairness and respect so that this becomes her normal. In school cultures where respect and dignity of all people are held as a priority, belonging is not used as leverage for social control. People are held accountable for protecting other human beings. Surround her with systems and people who are loving and value diversity. The values she learns from these role models will influence her beliefs and behaviours.

SUMMARY OF KEY POINTS

- Embed your daughter within fair and inclusive school systems which do not endorse status hierarchies.

- Remind her that every young person is equally worthy and belongs, even if they don't fit in with the group norm.

- Encourage her to have the courage to embrace her imperfections and seek connection and belonging.

PART 2

7-STEP GUIDE:
Healthy Relationships, Likeability and Limitless Girls

Power Over Peers

Cruelty is cheap, easy, and chicken shit.
– BRENÉ BROWN

Gateway behaviours involve small, inappropriate acts conveying contempt or dominance, such as ignoring, eye-rolling, laughing at someone, or displaying negative facial expressions. These behaviours occur when girls fight with each other, show arrogance, are being mean or expressing anger. Elizabeth Englander, a professor of psychology at Bridgewater State University, describes how adults often consider gateway behaviours to simply be relatively harmless minor transgressions. As such, their motives are also presumed to be innocuous. However, when gateway behaviours are continually used, the impact on the target can be significant. Whilst gateway behaviours do not necessarily mean that bullying is happening, bullies do use gateway behaviours.

'Hey, Bella. Do you know where gym class is today?' asked Lilly.

Bella continued to look straight ahead. Her eyes stared right through Lilly into the distance, but she paused long enough for Lilly to know she had heard her question and had chosen not to answer. It had been months since Bella had started to deliberately exclude Lilly, and by this point, Lilly just wanted the ignoring to end.

Lilly repeated, 'Bella, do you know where the gym class is?'

Bella's face remained motionless as she grabbed her bag and walked away. Before leaving, her nose wrinkled and a flash of a sneer dimpled her cheeks.

As Bella walked away from Lilly, she saw Ava. Bella's eyebrows raised and her eyes grew large with excitement as she grabbed Ava in a performatively warm embrace and exclaimed, 'How are you, beautiful?' Bella and Ava laughed as they walked away together.

Unless parents and teachers identify gateway behaviours as being unacceptable, bullying can happen in plain sight without being identified or sanctioned. Gateway behaviours also create maladaptive social environments which are harmful to all students by normalising hostility.

BULLYING

Just as bistrategic control is linked with relational aggression, it is also linked with bullying. Bullying is different from social cruelty in that the cruelty is repeated and deliberately designed to hurt or intimidate someone who is in some way less powerful. Less powerful girls do not have the same level of social support or status to defend themselves. Bullies tend to have high self-esteem and are competitive and socially included. Bullies take on the role of a judge in determining the worth of others and dishing out the punishments.

The rewards from bullying include increased status, dominance and control of the peer group. Bullies control peers through punishment for non-conformity. Bullying can be a source of fun and excitement within the group. With time, a girl who bullies may find it increasingly easier to remove the normal emotional restraints that prevent the infliction of harm on others. With repeated experience, a girl can find pleasure in taking the risk of bullying and testing the limits of how far she can go, accompanied by the potential danger from exposure or reprisal.

Studies in Western countries estimate that about 5 to 10 per cent of youth engage in chronic bullying behaviours and approximately 10 to 25 per cent of youth have been bullied. Bullying is not a fight between friends and it is not normal adolescent behaviour. Studies indicate that the youth targeted by bullies tend to be different from the cohort norm somehow, have a disinclination to fight back or fight back ineffectively, have a social quirk or less social support. This profile makes sense if you consider the targets of other forms of mistreatment. For example, thieves can choose any house to steal from; however, they may prefer those houses that are easier to access because of isolation (not part of a neighbourhood watch) without strong security (no bolts on windows and doors).

SELF-PREOCCUPATION

Common patterns of thoughts underlying bullying behaviour involve a fixed mindset of superiority and entitlement. There is a tendency for those who bully to consider that they are special, placing their feelings and rights above other people's. They instead see others as a means to achieve their own personal goals and they afford themselves rights that they do not extend to anybody else. People who engage in high levels of bullying behaviour will be drawn towards people who support or follow, rather than challenge, their willingness to demean others. There may be a tendency towards excessively driven and perfectionistic behaviour to demonstrate worth, which may present in varied domains such as academic achievement, appearance, sport or health.

The presence of high self-esteem may contribute to better than average self-promotion and public performance. Whilst this may seem like an advantage, our daughters don't have to think that they are more important than others and have overconfidence in their abilities to work hard and achieve. Self-esteem too often depends on social approval or external markers of success, which can lead to constant social comparison and ego defensiveness. Needing to be better than others can lead to traps of narcissism.

A recent meta-analysis of 842 studies found adolescent bullying behaviours are related to callous-unemotional traits, narcissism and impulsivity. Callous-unemotional traits refer to a lack of caring about others, characterised by low remorse and low empathy. Narcissism relates to beliefs of being better than others and behaviours striving for prestige and admiration. Narcissistic traits, like Machiavellian traits, are represented in the dark triad, a term that refers to three overlapping core socially aversive traits: narcissism, Machiavellianism and psychopathy.

The culture of focusing on self-preoccupation and self-esteem, may be influencing an increasing incidence of narcissism in our youth, as outlined by Jean Twenge and Keith Campbell, authors of *The Narcissism Epidemic*. Narcissistic behaviours are found in many areas, including charity work, where a girl can portray herself as great and obtain admiration through assisting. Altruistic actions towards others who can reciprocate, support plans for securing the rewards of attention, accolades and future social obligations from others. These traits exist on a continuum.

Brené Brown, a shame and vulnerability researcher, encourages us to consider that the narcissistic pattern of grandiosity, need for admiration, and a lack of empathy is underpinned by shame. When looking through the lens of vulnerability, these behaviours may indicate a shame-based fear of being normal or ordinary. Certainly, girls receive messages that suggest an ordinary life is meaningless. Are our girls so afraid of not being adequate to be noticed, loved, belong and have a sense of purpose, that they scramble to prove their worthiness through status? Narcissistic behaviours may be an attempt to overcome and provide protection from being ordinary, but ultimately lead to more disconnection and pain. There is a difference between doing something that matters and the drive to be noticed as extraordinary.

Sharon Salzberg, a teacher and central figure in the field of meditation, aptly notes that self-preoccupation 'admits no real connection to other people or the world around'. Instead, it is restrictive and limited. It asks:

- What do I have?
- What about me?
- How am I going?
- What is in it for me?
- How do they see me?
- How will they serve me?

CYBERBULLYING

Shortly after lunch, reception phoned my office to ask if it was okay to book Lilly for an appointment at the end of the day. I had not seen Lilly since she finished high school five years earlier and she was dealing with high levels of relational aggression. I was eager to hear how she was going since finishing school.

Lilly had not been alone in her harassment. The social environment at the school Lilly attended had been the topic of group clinical psychology supervision meetings at my offices for some time. One of my colleagues had phoned the school to express her concerns about high levels of bullying amongst the cohort. The school executive quickly dismissed this feedback.

Walking into the waiting room, I saw Lilly had grown into an elegant young woman with long wispy brown hair and a wide smile. I could tell she was wearing a work uniform from the writing on the front of her shirt.

I waited until Lilly was seated in my office before asking how she was.

I listened intently as she described the last five years. She worked overseas for one year, completed a four-year health degree and was now working full time. She had a great group of friends and was going well overall.

I was so impressed with Lilly's achievements, especially because I had been privy to the background of just how tough things had been for her five years prior.

'What brings you back to meeting with me?' I queried.

Lilly's eyes clouded over, and her cheeks blushed with anger as she looked at the ground.

It turned out that last week, Bella, the primary abuser from high school five years earlier, had enlisted her friend, Ava, to post a video mocking and laughing at Lilly on Instagram. Bella was the lead actress pretending that she was Lilly, while Ava filmed and posted the Instagram story.

'So, girls that are now in their mid-twenties and you haven't seen in five years created and posted a video designed to degrade you for their entertainment?' I double-checked I had heard correctly. Lilly slowly nodded.

A common motive perpetrators provide for cyber aggression is that it is for fun and believing that they are taking on a role of social importance. Bullying and cyberbullying are intertwined. It is most likely that those girls who engage in online cruelty are behaving similarly in face-to-face interactions, as was the case with Lilly's perpetrators.

Lilly had seen the video about half an hour after Ava had posted it, and she contacted Ava directly through

Instagram, asking for the removal of the video. When Ava did not take it down, Lilly's mother also messaged Ava and Ava's mother to remove the video. Ava responded to Lilly's mother with defiance, and Ava's mother did not respond to Lilly's mother at all.

However, involving Ava's mother achieved the goal and the video was down within 15 minutes.

'How are you now?' I asked Lilly.

Lilly responded with her jaw clenched. 'I had nightmares for a couple of nights. In my dreams, the girls are attacking me and I am trying to fight them off. I wake up sweaty and shaking.'

Ava had contacted Lilly the following day by text, most likely at her mother's request. The message said 'Sorry' and then progressed to deny that the video was hurtful and criticised Lilly for involving her mother.

'The apology was another attack,' Lilly recounted.

'You had every right to make sure that Ava removed the video, and your harassment stopped.' My tone of voice meant I was not mucking around. If this were a school situation, school officials are best placed to deal with bullying behaviours rather than directly contacting parents. However, as Lilly's perpetrators were no longer in school, this was not an option.

When a person high in narcissistic traits has boundaries enforced or is criticised, a strong defence will likely be mounted, and possibly a counterattack. Girls high in social dominance justify social practices that enhance social inequality through hierarchy legitimising myths. This somewhat protects their privilege and the privilege of their group. They don't like being treated like everyone else and consider this as undermining. When they no longer receive attention, admiration and the special treatment they believe they are entitled to, their happiness quickly becomes anger.

Cyberbullying is the most devastating form of social abuse a girl can experience because of its speed and spread. A girl can be attacked at any time or place and the messages often reach many people, but at the same time, it is unknown who exactly has seen it. This exacerbates adolescents' sensitivity to being watched by others or a judgemental imaginary audience. It is most effective at harming the target by weakening her sense of worthiness and her confidence.

SELF-SERVING BIASES

Moral disengagement describes a group of errors in thinking that predict bullying behaviour. These errors in thinking represent a series of self-serving biases which allow someone to harm another person while keeping a high opinion of themselves. The transgressor presents the information to themselves slightly distortedly, much like a defence lawyer trying to get a person out of jail by arguing extenuating circumstances. In contrast, a judge considers all of the information before them objectively and fairly. It is for this reason that mostly ordinary people perpetrate harm. Decades of research have identified the banality of motives that typically lead to mistreating others.

Psychologist Albert Bandura's social cognitive theory describes moral disengagement under four broad categories. In one category, the harm to others can be reconstrued as necessary for the greater good. The transgression is described using euphemisms and moral language and presents the damage as trivial by comparing it with worse actions. Alternatively, a person may deny their responsibility in harming another by justifying the harm as determined by other circumstances and minimising their contributions. Excuses may include that they are following their higher status peers or the leaders, or they are just following group rules. Another category involves distorting the consequences of the transgressions by minimising the impact and making light of the situation.

The most common moral disengagement technique associated with peer cruelty involves the tendency to criticise the victim, also referred to as dehumanising or victim-blaming. The perpetrator reframes the mistreatment as an altercation with someone she didn't like who deserved the mistreatment. By distorting the truth and minimising her own wrongdoing, the girl perpetrating the harm can present convincing arguments of her innocence to herself and others, keeping her self-esteem and public reputation intact. Some examples of moral disengagement include:

- 'I'm being loyal to my group who has good reason for doing this.'
- 'You can't blame me if others are doing it too.'
- 'It was a rational response.'
- 'We did not physically attack her; we just made some comments.'
- 'She is stupid/silly/mean and deserves it.'

- 'She should not have annoyed me.'
- 'There were good reasons at the time.'
- 'It was just a bit of fun.'
- 'I didn't hurt anyone; she is just a complainer.'
- 'The harm was small.'
- 'I said I am sorry; now she really should get over it.'
- 'It is just what girls do; it's the way it is.'
- 'It will toughen her up.'

Moral disengagement is like an *on-off switch* where thoughts about mistreating others can be selectively activated or deactivated. When the switch is flicked, errors in thinking override the moral frameworks which usually prevent the mistreatment of others. Unfair behaviour is consequently justified, reframed and rationalised. The most common circumstance of flicking the switch is when the injustice happens to someone outside of a person's group and the individual or their group are on the receiving end of advantage. There is not a moral knowledge problem, but a problem accessing morals in complex situations such as differentiating moral transgressions from social conventional rules.

It takes sophisticated moral development to imagine and experience mistreatment through another person's eyes. It also takes advanced insight to notice your thoughts without believing that every thought is true and to understand how privilege changes your version of reality. Moral disengagement effectively shuts down the human emotion of guilt, which typically guides people to behave morally. It facilitates a lack of empathetic concern for others rather than a lack of understanding that another person is distressed. It's the difference between seeing someone with 'cold' eyes or 'warm' eyes.

The good news is that errors in moral thinking are malleable and can change through modelling and moral conversations, referred to as moral induction. Noticing and correcting errors in thinking related to treating other youth fairly will help girls develop more complex moral reasoning. A girl can feel angry or find something humorous about another girl. Still, she must learn to regulate her emotions and never intentionally treat someone disrespectfully, regardless of what her group is doing.

RISK-TAKING BEHAVIOUR

Bullying tends to peak at ages 12 to 15 and declines by the end of school. It is crucial to recognise that girls are not fixed entities but complex, ever-changing beings with a range of possible behaviours. Social cruelty is a behaviour that girls can grow out of as their cognitive, emotional and social processes mature during this developmental period. Self-focus is often a transitionary adolescent developmental phase. Most girls will learn the importance of treating others respectfully as they grow older; however, some will better mask abusive behaviour and some will continue the behaviour into higher education and adulthood.

One longitudinal study of relational aggression conducted by Sarah Coyne, a professor of human development, found that 88 per cent of youth show low relational aggression levels that decrease with time. In contrast, 12 per cent enact increasing aggression as a normative and stable part of their social functioning into young adulthood. For this group, the normalisation of mistreating others can lead to lifelong difficulties in personality traits and relationships and is related to anxiety, depression, antisocial behaviours and loneliness. A girl can get *stuck* in status pursuits and engaging with others in dysfunctional ways.

I wanted to check on Lilly the following week to see how she was feeling. She arrived flustered with her handbag overflowing with papers from work but settled herself once she was in my office.

She smiled and nodded as I checked off a self-care list: Sleeping? Eating? Friends? Fun? Exercise? Mindfulness? 'Yes, I'm doing okay,' she replied.

Lilly described anxiety as her main symptom. She had a general feeling of being unsettled most of the time and her heart raced when she thought about the social media post and who might have seen it. Lilly also noticed that she was checking social media on her phone regularly to ensure there were no other posts about her. She had been distracted at work and when she was with friends. I knew that it would take her a little while to feel safe again.

Lilly and I reviewed ways to put boundaries up around future harassment, how she could curiously question thoughts that might lead her to become more anxious and how she could respond to anxious body sensations mindfully and by slowing her breathing.

Lilly's self-protective social media checking had included following what the perpetrators were posting so she could quickly act if it involved her again. Through this process, she learned something unexpected and puzzling.

'Ava's posts are copies of another girl's posts.' Lilly's comment was phrased as a question, and she tilted her head to the side, looking to me for a response.

'There is an older girl I follow on Instagram named Amelia. When Amelia posts, within a day, Ava posts something very similar. Ava's outfits, poses, colours and wording on the post are all very much the same as Amelia's.'

Lilly explained that she also learned that Ava, who was not a friend of Amelia's, watched and replicated many aspects of Amelia's life. She sought out jobs in Amelia's workplaces, bought a similar car, changed gyms to Amelia's, dressed how Amelia dressed and so on.

Exploring self-identity during adolescence is normal and copying others is a way to learn more about your preferences. However, when this is excessive and persists into adulthood, it can represent a problem. A girl can be so fused with hierarchically viewing people that she does not know or cannot see clearly to develop her own identity. Her opinions, interests, choices and goals merely reflect an ideal of status with which she is merged. She may repeatedly seek out higher-status others, like a satellite in the orbit of a star.

The risk is that pursuing status can become a narrow focus, with addictive qualities. Girls can feel envious of others whom they perceive as having one up on them in some way. If someone gets more than them, it feels like they get less. An excessive focus on status puts girls at risk for a wide range of future problems, including depression and other addictions. Whilst upward status comparisons can motivate a girl to emulate another to improve her status, it can also promote envy and pleasure at others' misfortune, facilitating downward comparisons to regulate shame.

Bullying and manipulation signify that a girl is engaging with peers and adults in dysfunctional ways. The focus on status will leave a girl with less real closeness or authentic connection with others. When status becomes more important than people, a girl can lose her understanding of the inherent value of people. Learning to get along with others as equals is an essential human skill. When missing, this is both the cause and consequence of loneliness.

SELF-COMPASSION

Self-compassion is a tool for our daughters to be kind to themselves whilst accepting emotional pain as part of a shared human experience. Being human is not about being better than others. It is not about judgements and evaluations to bolster self-esteem and ego. Instead, to be human is to have strengths and weaknesses. Wins and losses, successes and failures need to be separated from a girls' sense of self-worth. Instead of focusing excessively on her achievements, focus on who she is and her acceptance of imperfections.

If another parent complains that your daughter has been abusive, try not to be defensive, but instead start a conversation with her about what happened. If you learn that your daughter has mistreated someone, talk to her about it in a curious and compassionate way. Whilst it is essential to intervene and for your daughter to own her mistakes, using shame to change her behaviour is not helpful.

It is important that girls develop good moral codes and the self-compassion to be accountable, apologise and make amends. She needs to believe that she can and will do better. Discuss ways in which your daughter could remedy the situation. Maybe she could do an act of kindness for the hurt person. Help her find ways of catching herself before she behaves in demeaning behaviour again.

Taking an accepting approach to weaknesses and mistakes can help counteract shame, self-deprecation and defensive self-enhancement. Accepting herself as human and treating herself with warmth reduces a girl's threat perception, leading her to have more realistic self-appraisal and facilitating her growth. Self-compassion is more likely to help your daughter flourish through treating herself and others well.

In this book, seven steps are suggested to support your daughter to build healthy relationships with others, facilitating likeability and contributing to her overall flourishing. Some of the steps have a more obvious and seemingly direct link with strengthening authentic relationships. In contrast, other steps promote girls' growth as a foundation for their connection with others. The first two steps aim to increase girls' self-compassion.

STEP 1

BUILD SELF-COMPASSION INSTEAD OF SELF-ESTEEM

Step one supports girls' acceptance of themselves with kindness. When girls are compassionate about their weaknesses and understand this to be a part of shared humanity, they will better manage feelings of shame. If a girl has mistreated another girl, self-compassion will help her learn from her mistake and do better.

Below are some ideas for moving towards self-compassion and away from self-esteem.

- Talk to your daughter about which aspects of herself impact her self-esteem. These might include her appearance, fashion, athletic ability, grades, popularity, etc. Then, on each aspect, explore the following three questions adapted from Kristen Neff, a leading researcher on self-compassion:

  - Is this important for feeling connected with others (verses feeling better than others)?
  - Is this important for being healthy (versus being perfect)?
  - Does personal worth come from being human (versus being special)?

- Explore self-compassion and what it means. Perhaps you could help your daughter develop insight into her level of self-compassion by completing Neff's Self-Compassion Scale (SCS) which is suitable for girls 14 years and older and is available at https://self-compassion.org/. This website also contains self-compassion exercises and guided practices.

Own Your Story

What we achieve inwardly will change outer reality.
– PLUTARCH

Rejection and social cruelty are not rare events in adolescence. Social cruelty can result from mistakes and thoughtlessness. For example, a girl can behave carelessly or be angry and say something unkind rather than talk about a problem. A girl's perspective-taking, problem-solving and communication skills are still developing. So, whilst unkind behaviours between girls is upsetting, it is normal for girls to experience social problems and the learning derived from these experiences can be productive. Sometimes deciding to ride it out and focusing on repairing friendships and making new friendships is the most helpful way to proceed. When facing low levels of social cruelty, girls can learn valuable skills that will prepare them for adulthood. For this reason, it is often beneficial for a girl to manage difficulties independently, with the background of our love and support.

The context also influences the extent to which a girl is likely affected by social cruelty, more so than the severity of the attack or even her initial reaction. Your daughter will be much less affected if she is not already dealing with other stressors, such as being socially isolated or experiencing problems at home. Check in with your daughter calmly about what else might be going on for her. Social cruelty has less impact and it is easier for her to recover when she feels supported and has good friends.

The impact of social cruelty changes when there is repeated and targeted aggression against a girl. When relational aggression is frequent, even involving small actions, or if multiple youths are participating, the effect is more severe. Repeated attacks, especially in front of others, online public exposure, and anticipating future episodes, harm girls the most. In these cases, the response of adults needs to change. School professionals should be contacted to implement protective measures, as these experiences can lead to significant mental and physical health problems, which may persist even after the mistreatment has stopped.

TARGETS

Girls who stand out from their peer group norm in some way are more likely to be neglected by the group and targeted for social cruelty by aggressive girls. Reasons for being rejected by peers may include having a different appearance, having less or more money, minority ethnicity or sexual identification, poor or extremely high academic achievement, non-conformity to the dominant peers and holding different interests or ideas to the dominant culture. So basically, any characteristic or condition that stands out and does not fit with the normative culture of the group can lower a girl's status and leave her vulnerable to attack. In addition, girls become susceptible to attack when they withdraw socially or are emotionally reactive to peers.

As the peer group culture dictates the criteria for rejection, a norm violation in one group may not be a violation in another. Support for this proposition comes from studies showing that when the group norm is aggression, non-aggressive youth are rejected. In cross-cultural studies, youth with anxious and depressive symptoms are less popular in an individualist country but not in a collectivistic country.

Mental health problems may interfere with girls' relationships, resulting in their withdrawal from friends or behaving in ways that are less enthusiastic, less positive and less confident. A girl may also frequently seek reassurance within her friendships. By checking that everything is okay with her and the friendship repeatedly, the friend on the receiving end may start to avoid the relationship, which, in turn, may evoke more reassurance seeking. Friends may begin withdrawing as the relationship becomes uncomfortable. Mental health and peer problems tend to work in circular and reinforcing ways. The more friendship problems develop, the worse a girl feels, and the worse she feels, the more friendship difficulties arise.

Adolescence and young adulthood are high-risk periods for girls developing mental health problems, with three-quarters of all issues emerging during this time. The most common symptoms fall into the category of anxiety and depression. Very simply, anxiety may present as excessive worries, irritability and tension, whereas depression may present as low motivation, concentration difficulties, low mood and sleep disturbance. A referral to a clinical psychologist is helpful if a girl's symptoms persist for longer than a couple of weeks and interfere with her studies or relationships.

IMPACT

Social experiences have the power to change neurobiological systems and neuroendocrine reactivity. Cortisol responses can be compromised in girls, related to the extent to which they have experienced cruelty from peers, regardless of other stressful experiences in their lives. The hypothalamic-pituitary-adrenal axis (HPA) is a neuroendocrine system that includes emotions and the immune system. Alterations in this axis can result in poorer physical health. Studies of genetically identical twins who live in the same household show that differences in bullying experiences have dramatic negative consequences on multiple areas of wellbeing, including social, emotional, physical and academic domains.

Neural pathways and thought processes also change with social experiences. When mistreated, a person's optimism and level of trust in others diminish. As protective positivity biases are reduced, a girl may experience a form of 'depressive realism'. Some studies have found that after experiencing low status, a person tends to understand social information more accurately and in more meaningful ways. They can also become fairer at estimating their own skills and level of control over situations. This phenomenon is observable on brain imaging, with experiences of low status resulting in neural circuitry changes in certain brain regions.

Poor social experiences can result in several attribution biases, including hostile biases and rejection sensitivity biases. These biases occur with changes in neural wiring and begin as an adaptive neural defence. Being excluded by peers at the beginning of the year increases the risk of youth developing a hostile attribution bias or a tendency to assume others are hostile in ambiguous situations.

When a girl experiences hostility, she may continue to expect hostility in future interactions and react in kind. Likewise, when a girl experiences rejection, she may become oversensitive and respond to cues related to rejection. These biases can negatively impact relationships in a cyclic manner, making it more likely that a mistreated girl will have trouble in social relationships in the future. The impact of a girl's mistreatment is a risk factor for further mistreatment.

Being left out or mistreated by peers seems to disproportionately hurt girls, having a more pronounced impact on their wellbeing than boys. Girls feel more upset, sad and frightened after social cruelty. The more hurt a girl feels, the more likely she is to back away from her peers. And yet, following relational aggression, a girl needs to increase her social support. Friends are one of the most potent protection against attacks. Being with friends at lunch and when walking between classes can provide a buffer from bullies. Friends being there emotionally following an attack makes a positive difference to how a girl processes emotion.

REVENGE

Mistreatment hurts and can result in anger and urges for revenge. These evolutionary urges are accompanied by the activation of brain regions associated with pleasure. Revenge might show strength and prevent mistreatment in the future as others learn that one is not easy prey. Should one believe that they are in an unfair social system, they will more likely act on these urges as a form of self-help justice. However, revenge is a miswanting.

Revenge has high costs. When a girl tries to turn the tables on her tormentors, she may become a bully-victim, a term describing a youth who is a victim at times and aggressive at other times. Reacting aggressively increases a girl's familiarity with behaving in cruel ways to get what she wants and flicking the moral disengagement switch, increasing the likelihood of her acting in this way again. Secondly, despite what Hollywood movies on seemingly heroic vigilantes lead us to believe, responding aggressively to a socially dominant girl's cruelty is unlikely to create a fairer environment. The mistreated girl may be tainted as the aggressor and punished, increasing the perpetrator's power rather than diminishing it. Furthermore, a perpetuating cycle of revenge between both parties can escalate.

Even when people obtain revenge, it doesn't make them as happy as they predict. In studies where people could get revenge, they predicted it would make them feel better or reduce their anger, more than it did. In fact, revenge prolonged distress and thoughts about the hurtful transaction, which increased anger. It did not bring closure; instead, it perpetuated angry ruminations and distress, reducing life satisfaction. Thus, revenge is a paradox. We want something that will not contribute to our wellbeing. Instead, we can encourage girls to choose low-cost behaviours to protect their safety, confidence and sense of belonging. One of the most helpful strategies involves girls increasing their social supports both inside and outside of school.

Hurting others is a violation of the capacity of human beings to operate out of the good within them and this requires empathy. It isn't easy for girls to extend compassion when they are hurt, but this is where others can take over. Try not to encourage focusing on the person or people who caused the harm but rather the harm itself. Anger can be directed at the systems that created such behaviours, understanding its impersonal nature and that the perpetrators are trapped in a system, even as they trap others. Regardless, fierce self-compassion can protect girls by propelling them to actively care for themselves. If a truck were driving towards a girl, we would tell her to step out of the way. But we don't make the truck the enemy. Our daughters can be empowered to be active agents in their own lives by moving out of the way of harm.

SCHEMAS AND STORIES

Schemas are patterns of thinking. These patterns shape the stories we create about how worthy we are of love and whether we trust we can be safe with other people. It is normal for a mistreated girl to develop stories that fit her experiences to make sense of herself and the world. Unfortunately, mistreatment can skew a girl's patterns of thinking and can be coupled with self-defeating behaviours in the future. These self-defeating behaviours can be diverse. A girl can disconnect from others emotionally, become aggressive, or become overly dependent and clingy. Jeffrey Young's schema therapy provides an overview of common schemas or stories that may emerge following exposure to a poor social environment and are targeted in interventions.

These schemas include:

- **Emotional deprivation**: expectations that others will lack empathy, emotional care and protection
- **Social isolation**: expectations that others will exclude or isolate one because of inherent differences

- **Abandonment**: expectations that others will not be there when needing support and inclusion
- **Mistrust/abuse**: a lack of trust in others and expectations that others will intentionally mistreat, hurt or humiliate
- **Defectiveness**: feelings of shame and thoughts of being inferior, flawed or unlovable.

As well as social cruelty contributing to the formation of girls' unhelpful stories, pre-existing stories developed from other environments can mediate or change the experience and interactions of girls with their peers. Evolution has resulted in our minds having attentional biases such as excessively focusing on adverse events, with these events having a more substantial and more salient impact than good events. This tendency to ruminate conspires against girls.

Girls' meaning about the importance of being status popular can impact their wellbeing when experiencing peer difficulties. In a study of 158 girls, author and psychology professor Mitch Prinstein found ratings of peer importance influenced the development of depressive symptoms 17 months later. Ascribing high importance to peer status and caring about what peers think, as measured by responses to questions such as 'It is important for me to be popular with kids of my age', resulted in more distress to peer rejection. There is variability amongst girls about how vital peer status is, and girls who tend to be less impacted care less. Instead, these girls focus on their friends or say they don't want to be in the popular group. Having a small group of supportive, kind friendships is most protective for girls.

With the help of mindful awareness, girls can unhook from unhelpful stories about themselves and others. They can gently come back to the present and engage in actions consistent with beneficial outcomes for themselves and their peers. In this way, girls can choose the narrative of their own life stories.

Mindfulness meditation has many benefits for strengthening the brain by shifting the focus away from fear centres to regions of higher order thinking. When being present in a non-judgemental way, a girl's thinking and emotion regulation is improved, as is her sense of agency. Mindfulness is the foundation of self-compassion, which helps girls make room for discomfort and the complex emotions accompanying mistreatment, such as sadness, shame, fear and anger. Strength can come from vulnerability. When girls embrace their pain with kindness, it becomes more bearable as the activation of care systems reduces stress responses. Numerous studies have supported the significant protective role of self-compassion as a psychological buffer in the face of adverse life experiences. For example, self-compassion has been found to reduce the association between peer mistreatment and non-suicidal self-injury as a technique for coping with emotional pain. Mindful self-compassion is a healthy way for girls to feel and process emotional responses.

WHAT GOES RIGHT

Most of us can recall a school incident that evoked shame and changed how we think of ourselves and our worthiness. Cultures that devalue some people foster the highest level of disengagement as a form of protection. If we don't belong or feel a part of a system with our vulnerabilities, we don't contribute and we stop caring. Social rejection hurts in the same way as physical pain and results in disconnection, and a lashing out at others. Youth need to know that they are valued and a part of something bigger than themselves.

As stories are most malleable in youth, it is essential to ensure that our daughters have many opportunities to experience the benefits of connections with kind people. This does not mean that your daughter needs to have a perfect childhood. Instead, the quality of a girl's total experiences, rather than isolated events, will likely exert the most influence on her. In the words of Valliant from the Harvard Grant Study, 'What goes right is more important than what goes wrong'. Cumulative experiences of caring and respect can protect a young person and change their trajectory towards healthy connections and likeability.

'Hey, Mary … I had an AIDS test today,' Sarah told me over the phone.

'Oh no,' I thought. 'What have you done?'

Sarah and trouble paired together was nothing new. She was expelled from school by grade nine. Initially, Sarah was suspended after punching a girl. Although admittedly, the girl had hit her first. Then, she refused to pick up a piece of rubbish off the ground. The piece of rubbish was not hers and she objected to the sports teacher who walked 100 metres out of his way to single Sarah out for the job. You see, Sarah was denigrated to the lowest status within the school. She had dreadlocks, did not play netball like most girls, and was not cooperative with rules she thought were unfair.

'When you work at McDonald's, you'll need to cut your hair,' Sarah recalls was the last thing said to her by a passing teacher as she left the school grounds.

During the first couple of days at Sarah's new school, she struggled. She tells the story of doing flips in a physical education class and kids laughing. Sarah walked straight up to them and, muscling up, threatened, 'You laugh at me, and I'll give it to you'.

Her anger turned to horror as she saw her classmates' faces drop with confusion. At that moment, she realised that the flips looked ridiculous and her classmates were laughing at the scene, not at her. Sarah's environment had changed, but not her expectations of treatment or her defensive responses.

Sarah now works as an environmental scientist. She regularly visits her old school friends, including Susie, who also changed schools around the same time as Sarah and now works as a medical practitioner in rural Queensland. Contrary to the trajectory of antisocial behaviour mapped out by Sarah's teachers from the school that expelled her, she has no criminal or drug record.

The most important question is, what went right? One by one, Sarah's small group of friends changed schools to join her and she made new friends. In the new school, no-one tried to control Sarah's appearance or behaviour in unreasonable ways. Teachers respected her autonomy with a special mention to Mr Wilson, who went out of his way to include Sarah. Sarah decided on her own volition to get a haircut when she finished school and travelled to Europe to complete her first university degree.

So why did Sarah need an AIDS test? One morning on her way to work, Sarah saw a group of people surrounding a man on the ground. At a closer look, she noticed that the man was not breathing. She rushed in and administered mouth-to-mouth resuscitation until the ambulance officers arrived.

Afterwards, a man pulled Sarah aside and asked curiously, 'Why did you do that? He was homeless and looked like a druggo'. Sarah replied, 'I didn't see a druggo; I just saw a human being'.

GROWTH

Belittling experiences results in shame, the sense we do not live up to an ideal and we are unworthy of connection and belonging. Shame is an intensely painful feeling and can be stored as trauma. When shame dominates, the fear centre of the brain activates and vulnerability becomes too difficult. And yet, vulnerability is at the core of all feelings and embodies honesty and courage in the face of uncertainty, exposure and risk. Disconnecting from our emotions and vulnerability also moves us away from connection. By leaning into the discomfort, we can become more comfortable with accepting pain as a part of growth.

When your daughter treats herself with compassion, she may start to see opportunities that emerge from painful experiences. Whilst I do not wish pain on anyone, all experiences offer wisdom. Did any growth come out of the experience? We can explore whether some of what happened *to us* happened *for us*. Did the experience enhance or clarify personal meaning, perspective, reprioritising activities or new friendships? The paradox of adversity is that with loss, there is gain.

Research examining people's growth after adversity describes reports of increased concern for other people, a greater understanding and enhancement of strengths, increased appreciation of family and friends, increased openness to experiences of meaning and spirituality and changed priorities. Following justice-related experiences, a girl may gain strengths in justice sensitivities for others, further opening her mind and heart. Courage, compassion, and connection create a light that owes its existence to the dark. Your daughter's most remarkable growth can come from her darkest times.

DEFENDERS

There are far fewer defenders than we would like to admit. In surveys, most girls say they would defend a target of cruelty, but the reality is most girls do not. Some girls play the role of the assistor of the aggressor by laughing or joining in, whilst others just observe without intervening. However, observers who do nothing increase the perpetrators' and other bystanders' beliefs that their behaviour is acceptable.

Defending is moral conduct that arises out of compassion for another. Compassion means to *suffer with* another person. While it is much easier for your daughter to defend girls from social cruelty in her friendship group, it takes a more sophisticated skillset to support girls outside her group, especially those attacked by her group. A girl's identity becomes affiliated with her group and she will instinctively care less about out-groups. Whilst girls understand the harm from social cruelty, most girls will choose the benefits of group membership and identity to maintain existing friendships and status and protect themselves from becoming isolated or targeted. Girls who do not call out cruelty may also benefit by keeping to the social norm of staying loyal to their group. Defenders are different in that they make decisions to act based on moral principles rather than group-based concerns.

In looking more closely at defenders, recent research outlines the importance of empathetic or compassionate anger. Defenders get angry. In fact, a girl who feels angry will be five times more likely to defend others than girls who do not. Why do defenders feel angry? Firstly, they recognise the mistreated person's distress. Secondly, they understand the unfairness. Thirdly, they take responsibility for helping other people's wellbeing. Fierce compassion can empower girls to say no to what they know is harmful. The challenge is to help defenders use anger skilfully.

Skilful defending focuses on the target of cruelty as being the crucial person for attention and support. A girl can give the target eye contact and make it clear from her body language that she notices and disagrees with the transgression. She can let the target be in control of how she might assist. Does the target need help to get away? Your daughter can check in with the target after the incident and reiterate that she has a right to be treated respectfully. She can provide comfort and encourage her to talk to her friends and trusted adults. Our girls need to know that protecting peers from mistreatment is always necessary and appropriate.

STEP 2

BUILD SELF-COMPASSION AND OWN YOUR STORY

Like step one, this step involves increasing self-compassion. In step one, we looked at how self-compassion can help a girl accept both her strengths and weaknesses to facilitate a commitment to treat others respectfully. Step two involves developing compassion around painful emotions when she is the target of cruelty, as a way to heal and untangle from unhelpful stories.

Self-compassion is key because when girls are able to be loving with themselves around feeling pain, they are less likely to react harshly and disconnect. Instead, with the experience of empathy, girls can reach out and connect with support. Your daughter needs to heal with others by knowing that she is *not alone* when sharing her experiences of shame following cruelty. Helping girls understand that many others have experienced the same struggles, with gentleness and care, is the key to resilience from shame. When painful emotions are accepted with kindness and unhelpful stories are observed without fusion, girls can focus on doing what needs to be done to increase social support.

We want our daughters to know that they are worthy and to embrace their imperfections and vulnerabilities. We want them to know that their self-worth is not changed regardless of what happens to them. We want them to feel a deep love and compassion for themselves and others, to value respect and belonging, and to have courage to show up authentically in a rapidly changing world. Our daughters can come out the other side of mistreatment with more courage, compassion, connection and wisdom. Our daughters can write their own story around their shame experience; one which incorporates worthiness, hope, struggle and courage.

● The following mindfulness-based exercise involves a series of steps that can be helpful after a girl has been mistreated.

- Recognise painful emotions.
- Accept these emotions in a non-judgemental way – it is okay to be upset.
- Investigate the emotions – where can she feel emotions in her body? How does it feel? What stories come up with the feelings?
- Increase self-compassion – direct feelings and actions of kindness and care towards herself.
- Gently unhook from stories about herself and what other people think. She can celebrate her differences and imperfections, as this will help her connect to wider humanity the most. She can own her story and determine how it is going to end.
- Do something to connect with kind and compassionate peers.

In The Home

I will not teach or love or show you anything perfectly, but I will let you see me, and I will always hold sacred the gift of seeing you. Truly, deeply, seeing you.
— BRENÉ BROWN

What are the things in the home that can encourage girls to develop healthy relationships with their peers? Some general patterns emerge when looking at family factors and the quality of youths' relationships. Although these general patterns add to an overall understanding of youth behaviours, they do not necessarily contribute to predictions or assumptions about individual cases. Regardless, it is worthwhile to understand the possible home influences that may support an adolescent's development towards likeability.

ATTACHMENT

The quality of the relationship we have with our daughters makes a difference in their friendships. Attachment refers to an emotional bond connecting a child with their primary carer. Attachment style refers to the strength and expression of the attachment, which is influenced by the child's experience of the carer as reliable and safe.

My introduction to observing attachment styles was from inside a cupboard at Yarm Gwanga. Yarm Gwanga is a university preschool translating to 'Place for Children' in the local Aboriginal Anaiwan language. The toddler room has a closet with a mirrored door, reflective on one side and transparent on the other. I stood shoulder to the wall in a cupboard that was barely big enough to fit me and the storage bags kept there, whilst observing parents and their toddlers interacting.

When watching parents drop off their toddlers, differences in behaviours emerged. Some children didn't seem to care and weren't concerned with saying goodbye to their mum or dad. And the mum or dad didn't seem to care too much either, talking to others or fumbling with their briefcases. In contrast, some toddlers threw a massive tantrum and parents looked frustrated with their toddlers as they struggled to separate from them. Whilst separation behaviours can be influenced by bad days and developmental stages, general interactions between toddlers and their primary carers provide insights into possible attachment styles.

The two main attachment styles are broadly known as insecure attachment and secure attachment. Very simply, secure attachment is when children feel safe in a warm relationship with their carer. Such children may be observed as being generally okay to say goodbye when separating from the parent. In contrast, insecure attachment styles may demonstrate compensatory strategies for emotion regulation and interaction and comprise insecure-avoidant and insecure-anxious subtypes. Children who are avoidantly attached may display behaviours such as ignoring or avoiding the parent, reflecting a lack of closeness. Anxious attachment may be seen through clinginess and excessive anger and distress when the parent leaves.

Bowlby and Ainsworth, both early researchers on attachment, illustrated the importance of a child's relationship with their primary carer for their emotional, social and cognitive development. When a child is insecurely attached, she is more likely to become emotionally dysregulated when distressed and experience difficulties forming close ties with others. Secure attachment provides a competent foundation for social challenges and social self-efficacy. Developing a secure relationship with a primary carer results in the child exhibiting more confident behaviours that enable exploration of their environment, improved stress management, improved problem-solving and more skilled social interactions with others.

During adolescence, attachment style becomes more complex and rigid in comparison to that of younger children. Girls become more active in maintaining their existing attachment framework in a transactional manner, with insecure frameworks making them more likely to develop negative interpretations and interactions. For example, insecure anxiously attached girls may be more sensitive and reactive to rejection cues, display over-eagerness to please, or engage in excessive reassurance seeking. These behaviours, in turn, may contribute to an increased likelihood of social difficulties.

Bistrategic resource control behaviours are associated with insecure-avoidant attachment. Insecure-avoidant attachment is not an avoidance of social interactions or engagements but rather an avoidance of deep ties with others. Despite high levels of prosocial behaviours and being embedded in social networks, those youth who use bistrategic control strategies tend to report more uncomfortableness with closeness, less trust in others and view relationships as secondary to underlying goal pursuits.

Attachment styles can play out not only in platonic friendships but also when girls start dating. Our childhood attachment style sets the stage for what we now know about the importance of secure functioning in adult relationships. Clinical psychologist Stan Tatkin describes the three attachment types as an anchor, wave and island. Secure attachment is compared to an anchor (stable in commitment), insecure-anxious is like a wave (generous and giving but fluctuating and can retreat angrily) and insecure-avoidant is compared to an island (independent and self-reliant). Sometimes, insecure attachment styles can result in challenges to healthy connections.

Adolescents do not need the same physical proximity to their parents as when they were children. Still, they can derive security from knowing that their parents are supportive even when not with them. This emotional closeness increases a youth's belief about being loveable, worthwhile, safe and capable. Parental sensitivity and emotional attunement continue to matter in adolescence and attachment style is changeable depending on the improvement or deterioration of important relationships.

Youth need connections with parents and improving attachment with our daughters in adolescence, in an autonomy-supportive way, is invaluable. The Harvard Grant study outlines the unexpected outcome of attachment on wellbeing across the lifespan, highlighting the power of a warm childhood. Waldinger noted that over 75 years ago, when the study started, 'no-one understood the importance of attachment and empathy'. Fortunately, we are beginning to understand now.

Whilst it is beyond the scope of this book to delve into the nuances of attachment with your adolescent, consider increasing your skills in this area if you think that your relationship with your daughter needs repair. The important overriding message is to notice and care about how your daughter feels. Find ways to spend one-on-one time with her every week, whether going for a walk or having morning tea. You don't need to say much. Listen deeply and look for the feelings underlying the content of what she says. Don't try to control or fix things for her. Communicate your confidence in her ability to work things out for herself. Teach her through your behaviour that you are reliable, consistent and available and that she matters to you. Be involved.

Having difficult conversations with our daughters can help them develop the skills to meet the needs of both people in relationships and negotiate conflict. Girls can be supported to maintain connections during disagreements by effectively communicating their point of view and showing empathy for others. Girls' mistakes are opportunities for closeness and warmth and to explore important issues. Understanding that people who love each other can disagree and work things out, or agree to disagree, is a skill that will positively impact their lives.

HOSTILITY AT HOME

It can be helpful to step back and take stock of how commonplace aggressive behaviour is at home. Families higher in conflict, parents with frequent angry outbursts and family relationships with less cohesion are all related to aggressive behaviours in youth. Authoritarian parenting styles, harsh punishments, low affection and high expectations and control are also linked to youth aggression. Psychological control and manipulation at home to gain compliance can teach girls to engage in similar behaviours with peers. A parent's control of a girl using withdrawal of love, invalidation of emotions and shame, is akin to relational aggression. These behaviours involve threatening connections and relationships to achieve a goal.

Like parent relationships, siblings' relationships matter. Sibling rivalry refers to infrequent acts of conflict between two siblings of equal power and these interactions can result in improved social and interpersonal skills. In contrast, sibling bullying is aggressive behaviour by a more powerful sibling due to age, size or status, which occurs repeatedly and is intended to cause harm. In a family environment of favouritism where there is a status hierarchy in the home, with one child having greater access to parental resources, such as attention and gifts, cruelty between siblings can have the function of maintaining favouritism or conversely challenging the position of bias. Sibling relationships are part of adolescents' social world and the roles, both aggressor and victim, tend to transfer from home to interactions with peers.

The more controlling and cold parents are towards their children, the more likely it is that they will grow up with a sense of insecurity and may focus on attaining a sense of worth by chasing extrinsic goals. When a parent places excessive importance on affiliating with prestigious organisations, such as a high-status school, sporting or religious association, the message can be given to girls that appearances matter more than people. Similarly, widespread altruistic acts forming contracts of social obligation for reciprocal material or social gains and status can result in healthy relationships being viewed as secondary to these goals.

'Hey, I've saved you a seat, Charlotte.' Harper patted the seat next to her on the bus as she simultaneously looked through Olivia as if she did not exist.

Olivia was overwhelmed with confusion. Her eyes fixed on Charlotte and her mind raced. She was having difficulty making sense of what she was seeing.

It was the third day that Charlotte had chosen to sit with the popular girls and ignore Olivia.

Before the summer camp, Charlotte and Olivia's friendship was very close. Charlotte confided in Olivia about her difficulties at home. Charlotte's family was prominent in the community, playing notable roles in the school, church and local business. The family was successful socially and financially, and Charlotte's father ensured that his wife and children did not jeopardise their status. Most aspects of Charlotte's life were subject to control and criticism by her father. Charlotte was miserable and struggling to cope. Olivia worried about Charlotte and spent time listening and providing support. However, once at the summer camp, Charlotte cared less about her relationship with Olivia and more about fitting in with the popular girls, including Harper.

'Harper is not very nice to me,' Olivia confided to Charlotte. 'She either pretends I don't exist, or she pulls a bad face in my direction.'

'Just ignore her,' Charlotte nonchalantly responded as she left Olivia on her own again.

Charlotte's advice to 'just ignore' her mistreatment was distressing for Olivia. Ignoring implies that we acquiesce to the circumstances of power imbalances, which can normalise power differentials and escalate mistreatment. On the other hand, when a girl is encouraged to ignore *and* is given support through behaviours such as defending and proactively including a girl, this is helpful. Demeaning behaviours often evoke shame and the feeling of being flawed or unworthy of respect. Shame happens between people, in a social context. Sharing our story with someone who responds with understanding and compassion heals shame. In contrast, minimising or invalidating a person who is sharing their hurt, because we don't like to feel uncomfortable, exacerbates their shame.

Olivia had essentially been placed in a marginalised position until returning home, at which time Charlotte again turned to Olivia for emotional support. The lack of emotional reciprocity was disconcerting for Olivia, as was the realisation that the person she had given so much was more interested in popularity than her good friend's wellbeing.

The problem with being motivated by status popularity is that the importance of friendships is tied in with the role others play for one's personal gain. Relationships switch from deep to shallow. The focus on status popularity and competitive prosocial behaviours undermine healthy interpersonal relationships by moving away from authentic self-expression. Healthy friendships involve love, empathetic concern and responsibilities to increase a friend's welfare without always increasing your own.

Girls' friendships that are too out of balance can take away from their wellbeing. When a girl excessively focuses on taking care of others' needs, as Olivia had with Charlotte, her own needs can suffer. Girls can be reminded that they too have a right to be cared about in relationships and that it is okay to set limits around self-sacrificing. The act of self-compassion also involves protecting oneself by drawing boundaries and saying no and providing care to oneself.

Adolescents tend to favour having many friendships over quality friendships; this trend changes as we grow older. Science supports the importance of high-quality relationships. The quality of relationships is more important than quantity when it comes to loneliness. Waldinger highlights 'the quality of the close relationships matters and not the number of friends' in predicting success. So, whilst your daughter will benefit from keeping in touch with family and friends, this alone is not enough. She benefits most from being authentic and sharing all of the rich layers and complexities of being human. To reduce loneliness, we must increase meaningful relationships.

We can give our daughters the message that they are loved and important as they are; they do not need to compete for special status, attention and admiration. Relationships are sources of love and should not be confused with admiration. If she does not understand this, she may unwittingly choose relationships with others who also focus on admiration rather than emotional connection. Or she may select relationships with warm and giving others, but proceed to take from them without giving back emotionally.

MODELLING

Lilly's mother phone pinged, and she looked away from the report she was writing to read the message sent to the group chat. The message was part of a parent committee messenger chat organising the final school dinner and dance. She had previously messaged and requested to the committee that a fair process be used to select the girls who would be given the esteemed roles of speaking during the night. Her message read, 'I loved last year how the speaking roles were pulled from a hat. What are your thoughts on following suit this year?'

'The girls have this under control,' Bella's mother responded. Lilly's mother felt the tension in her forehead and her eyebrows furrowed together as she read the reply. By 'girls', Bella's mother had meant Bella.

Bella chose herself and two of the girls from her socially dominant group to take the speaking positions. Bella and one of her friends, Sophia, took on the role of the official hosts for the evening, introducing the ceremony's events. Bella's other friend led the dinner prayer.

Bella's mother was also in charge of the seating arrangements for the tables. On the night, she and her husband sat next to the new school principal.

Later in the evening, William, Bella's formal partner, sat next to Lilly to say hello. Bella was annoyed and pulled him away to dance. William eventually made his way back to Lilly, at which time Bella's friend Ava spilled a drink on Lilly. Lilly felt the cold liquid trickle down her spine and, sharply turning, managed to see Bella and Ava high-five each other and laugh.

The status popular girls also controlled the music on the night. When a girl walked up to the music stand to request a song, Bella blocked her. On the occasion that a non-dominant girl's song managed to play, Bella stopped it mid-song. It was not that the music chosen was terrible. It was about the status popular girls enforcing and maintaining their power.

At the end of the evening, the status popular girls left to attend the after-party, an exclusive event to which only half of the graduating class had been invited. The subsequent pictures and videos streamed on various social media platforms all night and into the following week.

Bella and her friends' speeches successfully gained the attention of the new school principal, who asked them to speak again at the end of the year awards ceremony at which they would be receiving awards.

In a setting where status is valued, selective self-promotion and relational aggression can accumulate social and material rewards and social learning around entitlement. Parents who give the message, either implicitly or explicitly, that their daughters are entitled to special treatment can promote behaviours involving a lack of regard for others feelings, needs or rights. Modelling of such behaviours facilitates the rationalising of interpersonal exploitation. If parents give youth rewards for getting ahead of others at any cost, unfair behaviours aimed at getting what they want can be normalised in relationships.

It is unlikely that Bella's mother knew the extent of Bella's relationally aggressive behaviours. As relational aggression involves socially sophisticated and nuanced social interactions to control the perceptions of others, partly by concealment, it may also serve to conceal behaviours from parents. This is consistent with research indicating that those adolescents who report the highest level of secrecy from their parents also engage in the highest level of relational aggression. Unfortunately, a circular process involving greater secrecy and poorer relationships can develop and be maintained and reinforced.

To direct our daughters' trajectory towards likeability, we can focus on providing love rather than privileged allowances. We can set empathetic limits around any entitled behaviours and talk to our daughters about balancing their desires with fairness towards others.

MORAL LEARNING

Family attitudes and conversations around how people are treated, particularly people different from the dominant group, can influence a girl's moral development.

'Hey, Mum.'

'Just wait a minute,' I murmured as I looked at my phone.

I just received a text from my colleague Caroline asking about the mother-daughter retreats we are planning.

I knew there is an incredible venue near Byron Bay.

'Hey, Mum.'

'Hold on …' I replied with my eyes still fixed on the screen as I typed my response.

The word 'phubbing' describes the extent to which parents use or are distracted by their smartphones when they are spending time with their children. Whilst we all have moments of being too busy to pay attention to our girls, a group of researchers found a connection between parental phubbing and youth social cruelty. They suggested that a high level of phubbing can be experienced as exclusionary by youth. The notable mediating factor was the youth's moral disengagement, or how the youth thought about excluding others.

Parents can use moral disengagement techniques when they learn that their daughter has acted abusively towards peers. For example, some parents may engage in thoughts such as:

- 'The harm was minimal.'
- 'It's just girls being girls.'
- 'Other girls were doing it too, so it is not my daughter's fault.'
- 'It was over-excitement from the formal night.'
- 'She (the target) is annoying.' 'She overreacts.' 'No one likes her.'
- 'The final dinner dance worked better because of the decisions I made; we did a better job than they would have.'

From the earlier chapter describing moral disengagement techniques, you might be able to identify the techniques of victim-blaming, diffusion of responsibility and minimising from the list of justifications. The last statement reflects a justification 'for the greater good' and promotes a status hierarchy legitimising myth. All girls will do better after having more opportunities to practise skills and increase self-confidence.

In a study of 1500 students, conducted by Associate Professor Izabela Zych and her colleagues, youth who perceived their parents to disengage morally were more likely to disengage morally themselves and experience low moral emotions and high involvement in social cruelty. In addition, repeated exposure to socialising factors that promote aggressive scripts influences aggressive thoughts and behaviours. Overall patterns indicate an increased likelihood of adults with high levels of Machiavellian traits having children displaying higher levels of Machiavellian behaviours. Similarly, higher parental relational aggression is associated with higher youth relational aggression.

Regardless of our girls' opinion of a person, a group of people, or what others are doing, their task is to learn to behave fairly and respectfully. Morality is the conception of human rights, human welfare and human justice. Relational aggression is a moral infringement of justice and equity principles. However, moral rules can be distorted in the media and many other sources of information. When this happens, it provides an opportunity for us to have conversations with our daughters to clarify moral rules and improve their moral reasoning.

The important message is that an adolescent's moral development is a malleable social cognitive orientation influenced by external social contexts. Our relationships with our daughters, the behaviours we model and the conversations we have, can make a difference to a girl's trajectory towards likeability.

STEP 3

BUILD SECURE ATTACHMENT

Building a firm foundation of compassion and connection in our relationship with our daughter and in our home environment will help our daughters flourish. Our daughter's learning of courage, compassion and connection – the foundation of purpose and meaning – is learned by being experienced. Girls' first experience of this is within the family. A warm and empathetic environment characterised by emotional closeness and the fair and kind treatment of both family members and people outside the family, moves girls towards likeability. Kindness becomes the template for future relationships.

We must have the courage to learn and grow imperfectly with our daughters. On our journey we too can recognise our own 'fine coats' and model for our girls how to take off these coats and to make room for the discomfort of vulnerability. We honour our daughters when we interact with them as parents from a place of being enough. Sometimes it can be helpful to reflect on our own childhood attachment experiences to help build a secure attachment with our daughters. Acknowledge that to give our children a sense of compassion and acceptance, it is our responsibility to practise compassion and acceptance of who we are.

We can focus less on life distractions and more on creating deep, loving, respectful connections with our daughters. Dan Siegel refers to the four S's, which provide an excellent framework for increasing secure attachment.

● Consider the following questions about your relationship with your daughter.

- **Seen** – Do you see her deeply and empathetically?
- **Safe** – Do you avoid actions that will make her afraid or ashamed?
- **Soothed** – Do you help her deal with difficult emotions and situations?
- **Secure** – Do you help her develop an inner sense of wellbeing?

Tools for Flourishing

As is a tale, so is life: not how long it is but how good it is that matters.

– SENECA

The three steps outlined so far have focused on increasing your daughter's likeability, by encouraging self-compassion for mistakes and emotional pain, and enhancing your emotional connection with her. The next four steps described in this chapter promote flourishing by building a mindset of worthiness and abundance. An abundance mindset is fostered through increasing positive emotions with gratitude, connecting with purpose and meaning to something bigger, accessing strengths for accomplishing goals and appreciating interconnectedness and the inherent value of all people. These skills enable girls to flourish by enhancing their emotional health and relationships.

An often-related story helps explain that we have a habit of covering up our inner goodness and abundance with defences to protect us from harm. In Thailand in the mid-1950s, a statue of Buddha made from plaster and coloured glass was moved from the ruins of an old temple. During the move, the statue cracked, revealing glimpses of gold underneath the layers of plaster. Two hundred years earlier, monks had applied the plaster to protect the now 600-year-old solid gold statue from invading Burmese soldiers. The monks did not survive, but the valuable gold that hid within the statue was saved. The plaster and coloured glass protected the statue from harm; however, these coverings hid the truth of the magnificence of the inner core of the statue for a long time.

Just as the monks covered the inner gold, our daughters may cover their goodness to protect from the judgements of others and messages from society about what is important. These layers may build over time because of miswantings, misguided stories and mistreatment. The tragedy is that with each layer of covering, girls may identify more and more with the outer layers and lose touch with the inner gold. The layers separate a girl from others. Yet, even when the gold cannot be seen, it is still there. It shines through when she is grateful for the abundance around her, when she authentically connects with others, when she taps into her inner strength for a meaningful purpose, when she touches the lives of others with kindness and when her fierce compassion protects herself and others. With these qualities, a girl's radiance will be evident to herself and others.

GRATITUDE

In the words of Gandhi, 'There is enough for everyone's need, but not enough for everyone's greed'. Thinking about what you should or could have, but do not, comes from a scarcity mindset. In contrast, an abundance mindset is thinking that there is enough. One way to foster an abundance mindset is to focus on gratitude. Gratitude is about being aware of good things and appreciating them. The benefits of practising gratitude extend to an individual's wellbeing, their relationships and the wellbeing of the lives of those they touch.

Gratitude helps girls by reducing a sense of entitlement. When a girl is thankful for what she already has, instead of thinking about what she wants, she starts to experience a greater sense of wellbeing, better health and increased positive emotions, including contentment. Girls begin noticing the goodness within and around them. In seeing and appreciating the gifts they have received, a girl develops a sense of attachment to something bigger than herself. Gratitude is protective as it increases growth and facilitates the appreciation and use of gifts, even in challenging circumstances and during adversity.

How does gratitude deepen girls' connections with others and help them flourish? When a girl reframes her perspective to think that she has enough, she can think better of others. A scarcity mindset narrows a girl's attention to danger and threat. In contrast, gratitude widens awareness of connections. Girls start to notice the natural beauty around them and increasingly attach to the world and others. By thinking of the things for which she is thankful, new forms of value emerge, as well as the capacity to extend these gifts beyond herself.

Gratitude increases how much girls notice others, are thoughtful of others and help others. The power of appreciation amplifies when appreciation is expressed directly to others for something they have done. We tend to underestimate the positive impact this has, with people experiencing more joy than we realise. When your daughter acknowledges those who have helped her, not only will she herself flourish, but the benefits will extend to those to whom she has expressed appreciation. Many times, it is the small things that are the big things in life. When girls move from scarcity to enough, they start to experience the generative power of gratitude and grow with others from the generous acts of sharing gifts.

BUILD GRATITUDE

Building gratitude encourages girls to see the good in the world and embrace positive experiences and connections. To help our daughters tap into gratitude and become aware of the gifts surrounding them, we can talk about and practise gratitude at home when possible. Focusing gratitude on other people increases kindness and connection.

- There are many ways to practise gratitude, with gratitude best savoured by consciously noticing and lingering over the event to prolong and deepen the experience. Some ideas include:
  - Start a routine of sharing three good things every day at the dinner table to celebrate good moments.
  - Start a game of 'spot the helper' to draw attention to all the kind deeds others have done for your daughter or someone in the family by everyday people. Who are the people you are grateful for and who went out of their way to help? What did these people do?

- Your daughter might have a gratitude diary she writes in every night before she goes to sleep.
- If your daughter is on social media, you might start a family group chat where everyone can post photographs or notes about the things they enjoy and appreciate.

I live in a small city referred to as the 'city of four seasons' due to the beautiful but diverse nature displays, which never leaves me short of gratitude. Winter mornings are icy white, autumn brings bright orange, red and yellow leaves, spring bursts with green lawns and trees and summer is hot with the scented blooms of roses and magnolias. What beauty is around you?

SIGNATURE STRENGTHS

My daughter, Gabs, diligently working on her history project, asked me for help putting together our family tree. My husband, Paul, knew that his family had lived in Australia for many generations, but he knew little other details. Digging deeper, we learned some surprising facts. Our girls' great, great, great grandfather was John Foster, a boy of 14 years living in London when he was convicted of petty theft and deported to Terrible Vale Australia, 40 kilometres from where we now live. We knew the name of the ship John arrived on and his date of birth, marriage and death. It left us curious. These details were superficial, telling us nothing of real substance about him. Who was John Foster? What was his story? What characteristics or traits did he have?

When we think about our daughter, it is not her exterior layers or her fine coat that defines her. It is what lies underneath the surface. The unique combination of a girl's traits and how she expresses these traits represent her authentic self. A girl's signature strengths can capture her qualities or virtues over time and across situations. These strengths tell us something about what she cares about and who she is. Martin Seligman, a leading researcher in positive psychology, categorises signature strengths into six virtues and 24 domains, listed at the end of this section.

Besides the value of describing our daughters with the richness that comes from her signature strengths, these strengths also provide a vehicle for her flourishing. Our daughters can use strengths to help them achieve goals for growing and for responding to challenging experiences. Activating signature strengths improves problem-solving and coping. Strengths draw parallels with water. Water can show itself in many ways. Water can be a powerful jet spray, hard ice, mist, gentle snow, or soft drips. Water is flexible, moving and changing. So too, strengths can be experienced in many modes.

Numerous studies outline the advantages of accessing signature strengths, or gifts of character, for flourishing. When girls recognise, activate and connect with strengths, they will be happier, more productive and more satisfied with life. My doctoral thesis supervisor and UNE researcher, Nicola Schutte, performed a meta-analysis reviewing 14 studies and found robust support for the causal elements of accessing signature strengths in interventions for increasing positive affect, life satisfaction and decreasing depression.

In terms of improving our daughter's relationships, drawing on her signature strengths has the power to deepen her authentic connections with others. Firstly, knowing her strengths will help her improve positive emotions, handle friendship problems and increase intimacy with others more effectively. Secondly, accessing signature strengths is consistent with a worthiness mindset, as acknowledging and acting on strengths does not reduce another person's strengths or have a competitive focus. Her appreciation and respect for others will deepen to a more authentic level, as she is better placed to spot strengths in others. When another person is really seen beneath their 'coat', the understanding that is felt and created is a strong foundation for genuine connection and intimacy.

STEP 5

BUILD SIGNATURE STRENGTHS

Step five involves increasing a girl's use of her signature strengths. So, what can you do at home to help your daughter recognise and use her signature strengths? Below are some ideas:

- Review the 24 character signature strengths with your daughter and point out when you notice her using a strength. Encourage her to use her top five or so strengths in new and different ways flexibly and regularly.

WISDOM

Curiosity: Interested. Explores new things. Open to new ideas.
Love of learning: Masters new skills and topics. Systematically adds to knowledge.

Judgement: A critical thinker. Thinks things through. Open-minded.
Perspective: Wise. Provides wise counsel. Takes the big picture view.
Creativity: Original and adaptive. Clever. A problem-solver. Sees and does things in different ways.

COURAGE

Bravery: Shows valour. Doesn't shrink from fear. Speaks up for what is right.
Perseverance: Persistent. Industrious. Finishes what one starts.
Honesty: Authentic. Trustworthy. Sincere.
Zest: Enthusiastic. Energetic. Doesn't do things half-heartedly.

HUMANITY

Kindness: Generous. Nurturing. Caring. Compassionate. Altruistic.
Love: Warm and genuine. Values close relationships.
Social intelligence: Aware of the motives and feelings of others. Knows what makes others tick.

JUSTICE

Teamwork: Team player. Socially responsible. Loyal.
Fairness: Just. Doesn't let feelings bias decisions about others.
Leadership: Organises group activities. Encourages a group to get things done.

TEMPERANCE

Self-regulation: Self-controlled. Manages impulses and emotions.
Prudence: Careful. Cautious. Doesn't take undue risk.
Humility: Modest. Lets one's accomplishments speak for themselves.
Forgiveness: Merciful. Accepts others' shortcomings. Gives people a second chance.

TRANSCENDENCE

Appreciation of beauty and excellence: Feels awe and wonder in beauty. Inspired by the goodness of others.
Gratitude: Thankful for the good. Expresses thanks. Feels blessed.
Hope: Optimistic. Future-minded.
Spirituality: Searches for meaning. Feels a sense of purpose. Senses a relationship with the sacred.
Humour: Playful. Brings smiles to others. Light-hearted.

- Encourage your daughter to complete the VIA youth report, a free personality test that measures individual character strengths, available from https://www.viacharacter.org/

- Spot others signature strengths. In our family, we made a family tree of signature strengths. Notice strengths in people and use this knowledge to understand better another's perspectives, motivations and ways you can be supportive.

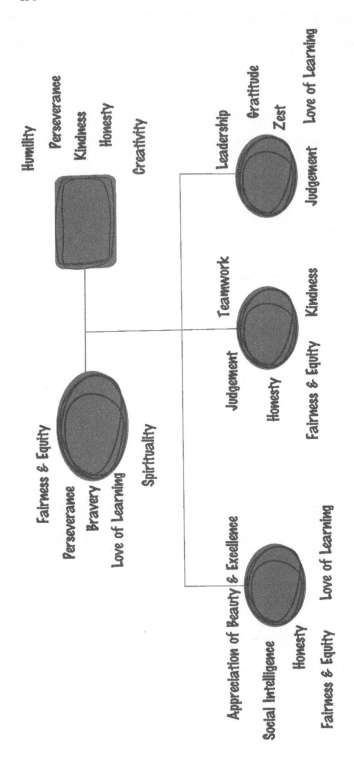

PURPOSE AND MEANING

When I was a young girl, I would travel to Chicago from Australia to visit my grandparents, aunts, uncles and cousins. The visits often involved meeting primarily strangers, and I was apprehensive about spending time with them. One exception was my great Uncle Joe. I wanted to know more about him. His body showed glimpses of the scars from his past, including whip marks and an identification tattoo. Uncle Joe had been a Corporal in the Polish Army when he was captured by the Nazis and held in a concentration camp until the end of WWII. As a young girl, I wanted to know about his journey. How did he survive? What helped him endure? Uncle Joe never shared these details with me. Perhaps he thought I was much too young to understand.

Viktor Frankl, a psychiatrist and Holocaust survivor, described glimpses of his experiences within the concentration camps in his book *Man's Search for Meaning*. Frankl observed that those prisoners that transcended their circumstances to care for and provide comfort to others developed a sense of meaning and purpose that gave significance to their lives and provided an inner strength and perseverance. This sense of purpose was derived from belonging to and serving something larger than the self. Having purpose and meaning changed how a person approached difficult circumstances in their life. With purpose, a person can choose their attitude despite facing seemingly insurmountable obstacles.

Finding purpose is like finding your roots. When you have good roots, a storm can toss you around without destroying you. Strengths are entwined with purpose and meaning. Strengths grow from having a purpose, which can buffer the experience of adversity, but purpose and strength can also grow as a result of adversity. Adversity can create a more vital and authentic purpose and contribute to growth by changing pathways and priorities.

When a girl uncovers the reasons underlying her goals and translates this into a coherent, meaningful story, her wellbeing, motivation and perseverance in life have the potential to be remarkable. So, what is purpose? Purpose relates to who your daughter is and what she values. What does she really care about? What makes her angry? What makes her happy? What would she like to change if she could? Adolescence is a great time for our girls to consider what they value and how they want to be in their lives.

Not all values have the same implications for wellbeing. The ancient Greek philosopher, Aristotle, distinguished hedonic and eudaemonic goals in the creation of purpose and meaning. Hedonic happiness refers to immediate gratification or pleasure, such as that derived from self-enhancing plans. Aristotle described a life of purely hedonic goals as akin to grazing animals pursuing pleasure from consuming and then resting. Eudaemonic happiness refers to being in touch with a true or inner self, which comprises self-transcending goals and serving something more extensive than the self.

People tend to have better emotional and physical health, such as lower pro-inflammatory responses, higher antibodies and even improved DNA when striving for self-transcending goals. When thinking about our transcending goals, parts of the brain in the prefrontal cortex, associated with decision-making, become activated. In this state, we tend to be better able to organise and change behaviours and are able to develop a future orientation and know in which direction we are going.

So, how do we help girls develop self-transcending goals? For a girl to start thinking about things bigger than herself, she will need to increase her openness to experience and be curious about the world. If she could stand where another person is, what would she see? What would she hear? What would she feel? When a girl is comfortable, it is more difficult to empathise with another person's suffering. Pushing herself outside of her circle of friends and what is known is one of the best forms of education available. The more educated about life she becomes, the wiser she will be in her choices about her purpose. Without this kind of education, a girl can take on goals and ambitions in the wrong direction for humanity.

At 18 years old, after finishing her higher school certificate, my friend Rebecca, got on a plane from Sydney to Buenos Aires, armed with her Lonely Planet guide containing the address of a backpacker's hostel. There were no mobile phones or internet at the time. She set off on a bus to the foothills of the southern Andes to Mendoza, where she met a ruthlessly pragmatic widow. Rebecca paid a small fee to sleep on the widow's pull-out cot in her living room for the next year, with the other five rooms of the three-story adobe mud house rented to students and workers from regional Argentina.

Rebecca improved her Spanish whilst working in a restaurant. That was where she met Andrea, a girl her age who had migrated to the city for work, leaving behind her newborn child. Rebecca recounted how hard Andrea and she worked for such little pay, how much Andrea missed her little boy, and the sacrifice Andrea made to send money home to provide for him.

This experience forced Rebecca to challenge commonly held stereotypes about people from lower socioeconomic positions. The people she lived and worked with were hardworking and intelligent. A lot about what happened to the people she met was about the context in which they lived. Rebecca had to confront certain assumptions about the circumstances of success. She described her realisation that prejudices can provide people with a bubble of safety to protect them from uncomfortable realities. She started to identify herself with the entire human race rather than a subset of people. Pushing herself to explore outside her group and familiar surroundings forced her to accept that people share more similarities than differences. Regardless of life circumstances, people were still people.

'It was a nice equaliser,' Rebecca said.

STEP 6

BUILD PURPOSE AND MEANING

Help your daughter flourish by encouraging her to connect with her values that guide her towards her goals. We can encourage our daughters to do the right thing, in the right way, for the right reasons. Below are some ideas for helping girls build purpose and meaning:

- Support your daughter to take a journey to make sense of who she is and what she cares about by spending time in the larger world and with different groups of people.

- Ask big questions such as, who is she? What does she want to do? And most importantly, *why* does she want to do it?

● Discuss what matters to her for her health, hobbies, future learning or career and relationships.

● Ask her what is the smallest possible achievable step she can take this week towards a meaningful goal? Then, put everything you have, within reason, into backing her.

COMMON HUMANITY

You might perceive a tree to stand on its own as a separate and distinctly defined entity. But when you look more closely, a tree has many links and subtle networks of relationships. Trees are influenced by and influence the rain, the soil, the air and the wind. A tree's root network is connected to other trees through underground fungal networks, sharing water and nutrients. Trees are connected and interdependent, and so are we.

Interconnectedness relates to the idea that there is no separation of ourselves and others. In very fundamental ways, humans are the same. We are all the same in not wanting to be hurt. Pleasure and pain, loss and gain, are the conditions of life for everyone. Everyone has unconscious urges, frameworks of thinking and emotions driving their behaviours. Everyone relies on everyone else in some way, and everything we do affects more than just us. How many people need to be doing their jobs well for us to go about our day? We couldn't exist without others. We are part of something much more significant than ourselves.

When a girl is focused on improving and maintaining self-esteem by filtering experiences through her ego, she is missing out on connecting with something much greater than herself. Creating a category in which she is superior paradoxically creates a contraction through closed rigid boundaries and separateness from others. In contrast, when your daughter connects on a level of shared humanness, winning and losing seems less critical and her world and sense of possibility expands. Success in others will not diminish her and she will better connect with other people's happiness. The joy is shared. When understanding interconnectedness, she understands that taking care of others is an inextricable part of taking care of herself.

Who do we see through?
Who has less power?

One of life's greatest tensions is accepting that injustice is commonplace. If we don't notice that some people are treated unfairly, then we are not paying attention. If we notice and decide not to care about them, we become part of the problem. Efforts to protect ourselves from mistreatment should extend to efforts to protect other people from mistreatment. This often involves interrupting systems and people that wield unequal power or control, which is harmful to everyone. The American philosopher Cornel West rightly commented, 'Justice is what love looks like in public.'

If in doubt about how to encourage your daughter to treat others, follow the Golden Rule: *If your daughter would not like it done to her, she should not like it done to others.* Equally as important, *she should not do to others what she would not want them to do to her.*

Whilst we can talk to our daughters about how the Golden Rule applies to her specific peer group, we need to widen and deepen the conversation to expose power inequalities in broader systems within our society. The Golden Rule is often forgotten when moral codes and philosophies are argued with abstruse doctrines, resulting in discrimination against some people or groups. When the culture of an organisation prioritises those with more power and the reputation of the system, whether that system be the family home, the school, or church, over the fair and respectful treatment of people, name it. We can talk about issues of systemic bias and take personal and collective responsibility to dismantle it. When it comes to social justice, every action matters, no matter how insignificant it may seem, and we can all be a part of it. Choosing silence and neutrality is choosing a side, as this helps the oppressor. It requires great courage, even as an adult, to make yourself vulnerable to a group moving in one direction and yet stand up to make the ethical decision.

Fortunately, our daughters are growing up in a period of accelerated resistance of people-powered movements overturning systems of 'power over'. We are increasingly intolerant of differential rules based on gender, race and sexuality. Instead of striving for 'power over' others, a girl can shift towards 'power with' others. Power comes from wisdom about equity issues and consciously constructing a new way forward, such as not falling prey to the bystander effect. Bystanders typically treat targets of mistreatment based on their status within the group. A girl can challenge that by noticing and caring about the suffering of those most vulnerable in her school. Understanding interconnectedness and common humanity can also help a girl understand the impersonal nature of relationally aggressive behaviours. Actions are carried out in a larger picture of causes and conditions. She can contribute to a more inclusive and equitable situation. Compassion can take the form of actions of kindness and protection towards herself and others. It is both the tender and fierce aspects of compassion that contribute to flourishing.

Compassion-based meditation can change the processing of emotions and empathy. Just as purpose and meaning can rewire the brain's neural circuitry and change blood flow to the prefrontal cortex, so can mindfulness. Mindfulness meditation enhances emotion regulation and immune responses. As well as resulting in objective changes to the brain structure, meditation affects aspects of our experience, including reducing subjective feelings of suffering and cultivating happiness, satisfaction and appreciation.

There are many versions of mindfulness meditation. Loving-kindness meditation is a strategy for increasing your own flourishing and spreading flourishing to others. The meditation typically starts by focusing on good wishes towards yourself and extends these wishes to others. In the first instance, the benefactor may be a friend who has been good to you, a friend who is doing well and a friend who has difficulties. These wishes of acceptance and goodwill continue to extend to all people and beings, whether known or unknown. Guided loving-kindness meditation practice often uses variations of the following phrases.

May I be safe, be happy, be healthy, live with ease.
May you be safe, be happy, be healthy, live with ease.

The practice of loving-kindness meditation can cultivate a girl's feelings of care and empathy for others, increasing her awareness of her interconnectedness and how her choices ripple outwards. Ironically, spending time alone in mindfulness meditation helps undo the perception that she is alone, instead fostering stronger connections and tolerance. Loving-kindness meditation reminds a girl of her relationships with the natural world and all living things and that all are worthy of kindness and respect.

STEP 7

BUILD INTERCONNECTEDNESS

Step seven for flourishing is to help your daughter understand and respect her common humanity and connectedness with the wider world. Move your daughter's thinking towards 'power with' rather than 'power over' others. Ideas include:

- Make time for a small mindfulness meditation as part of the daily routine

- Teach your daughter about historical events involving 'power over' where people mistreated each other based on classifying them into distinct groups such as culture, skin colour, gender or sexuality

- Teach your daughter to notice 'power over' behaviours in her peer group. How have some peers established 'power over' other peers? Encourage her to get to know peers from different groups to her own and to care about their difficulties

- If ever in doubt about how to treat others, discuss the Golden Rule. Would your daughter like someone to treat her in the same way?

- As a family, engage in random acts of kindness to increase her circle of care

- Increase family time in nature and with animals to foster connections with the natural world

- Model being attentive and interested in people around you and connecting in small ways such as with a smile and eye contact.

Limitless Girls

Limitless like the ocean are your excellent qualities.
– DALAI LAMA XIV

The steps outlined in this book are designed to help our daughters improve their friendships and flourish in all aspects of their life during adolescence. When a girl understands what is fair rather than being preoccupied with winning, and focuses on compassion and recognising the strengths that she and those around her have, her friendships become happier and more genuine. Although every friendship has its own challenges, being compassionate to herself and others can bring kindness to tricky situations and a caring, fierce force for everyone to flourish together.

Whilst adolescence may be a developmental period marked by rapid social change, the social dynamics of adolescence can also play out in the social arenas of adult life. Throughout adulthood, the qualities of compassion and fairness add to one's character, contributing value to relationships. It is likeability that predicts so many outcomes in the decades following adolescence, even after accounting for factors such as intelligence and socio-economic status.

Likeable adults work together to achieve great things and contribute to thriving workplaces without competing against each other. It is not the type of work a person does but the qualities they bring to their work that make the difference. Skills in likeability adds value to any workplace and contributes to growth over one's career.

The principles of likeable popularity and flourishing extend to success in leadership roles, whether the leadership role is within the school, as is the case with teachers and school administrators, or another workplace. Leadership is not about title, number of direct reports, or status. Rather, it embodies a set of characteristics and skills for finding possibilities and potential within an organisation and in the organisation's most valued resource, people.

Likeable leaders lead differently from high-status leaders. They make us feel safe from being demeaned, to bring out our best as we transform, create and fail. This process is the basis of innovation. Whereas high-status leaders tend to insert themselves into high-ranking positions and exert dominance while protecting their interests, likeable leaders make everyone feel valued by listening and creating fair group norms and harmony.

My sister, Katherine, is a lawyer who works as a CEO in the superannuation industry. When I ask her how she leads such a large number of people, she describes how she aims to gracefully 'move between the dancefloor and the balcony'. On the dancefloor, she describes being with the people of the organisation. Each person within the company is included and authentically valued for their unique contribution. When moving to the balcony, she must step back and create space to make decisions while continuing to be inclusive and transparent.

'The balcony is reserved for times when people need to know who is going to lead them through a storm,' Katherine explains.

A true leader is successful in situations in which those motivated by their status cannot be. Not only do diverse and inclusive workplaces contribute to the increased wellbeing of employees, but a growing body of evidence also concludes that these environments tend to generate higher revenue and greater profitability. Likeable leaders are the best leaders. The reality is that all girls are leaders when they know *where they want to go, how to get there, and believe they can do it.*

We should genuinely care about our daughter's likeable popularity and flourishing. Likeability is the key to success across multiple measures. Success is measured not by being at the top but by investing in the betterment of humanity, developing depth of character and enjoying genuine relationships.

So here is the question:

Given that likeable popularity is so powerful, why is this key to modern-day success effectively minimised in the upbringing of our daughters? Why is so little time spent teaching likeability to our girls?

A girl's superpower is her ability to take off her 'fine coat' so others can take off theirs. Through accepting vulnerability and responding to herself and others with compassion, a girl can better share 'power with' others, effectively amplifying her own. With likeability, a girl's world gets bigger, the way she relates to herself and others gets bigger, her creativity gets bigger, her sense of possibilities gets bigger and her heart gets bigger.

She is limitless.

ABOUT THE AUTHOR

Dr Mary Kaspar graduated with first-class honours and was awarded a doctorate in clinical psychology from the University of New England. She is the director of a private psychology practice where she works with adults and adolescents, both individually and through her online programs.

Dr Kaspar was born in Chicago in the USA and moved to regional Australia as a young girl, growing up as the second eldest of five sisters and two brothers.

She and her husband live in Armidale, New South Wales, with their three daughters and two Cavaliers.

As a psychologist and a parent, Dr Kaspar strongly believes that with insight and support, girls can grow in courage and compassion, so that they may walk alongside others, rather than stand over them. *The Popular Girls* is her first book, and was inspired by her passion to help families unlock the characteristics of their girls that can propel them towards future success and happiness.

If you'd like more information and resources to support your daughter's likeable popularity and flourishing, visit **thepopulargirls.org** website where you can register your interest for the online course for parents and carers 'Parenting for (Likeable) Popularity' and the fun online bootcamp-style course for teens 'The Popular Teens'.

ACKNOWLEDGEMENTS

This book would not have come about without the loving encouragement of my family and friends. To my daughters, Ashryn, Gabrielle and Georgia, who never fail to inspire me. To my husband, Paul, whose loyal, consistent support saw the journey of this book to completion. He is the most devoted partner and father to our daughters.

Growing up with my sisters taught me the value of authentic connection and fierce compassion for others. My sister, Henia, taught me that love is the fight for social justice and courage when facing unfairness. A special thanks to my sister, Katherine, and my daughters for their kindness and insightful feedback on the early drafts of the manuscript.

The manuscript was greatly improved by the feedback from colleagues in the fields of psychology and education. The book could not have evolved without the generosity and expertise of Dr Caroline Croft, Associate Professor Nicola Schutte, Professor Pep Baker and Dr Angela Page, for which I am boundlessly grateful. The book is also interwoven with the ideas and work of great psychologists who have informed my thinking and shaped my career as a clinical psychologist. Their work has paved the way for what is possible now.

This book incorporates the wisdom, adversities and strengths of the beautiful girls and young women who have touched my life over the years. It has been an honour to be a part of their journey, even if that has been in some very small way.

This book is inspired by and celebrates all girls and young women.

THE NEXT STEP...

If you are interested in further investing in your daughter's flourishing and likeable popularity, the next step is to sign up for more information at **thepopulargirls.org**

- The **Parenting for Popularity** course offers insights and practical solutions to successfully integrate strategies for flourishing and likeability into your parenting and home environment.

- **The Popular Teens** online course is a fun, online bootcamp led by a clinical psychologist and designed to teach teens skills that are proven to support wellbeing and likeability.

REFERENCES

Alba, J., Calvete, E., Wante, L., Van Beveren, M-L., & Braet, C. (2017). Early maladaptive schemas as moderators of the association between bullying victimization and depressive symptoms in adolescents. *Cognitive Therapy and Research, 42*(1), 24–35.

Australian Psychological Society & Swinburne University. (2018). *Australian Loneliness Report.* https://psychweek.org.au/wp/wp-content/uploads/2018/11/Psychology-Week-2018-Australian-Loneliness-Report.pdf

Barry, C. T., Kerig, P. K., Stellwagen, K. K., & Barry, T. D. (2011). *Narcissism and Machiavellianism in youth : Implications for the development of adaptive and maladaptive behavior* (1st ed.). Washington, DC: American Psychological Association.

Bayraktar, F., Machackova, H., Dedkova, L., Cerna, A., & Sevcikova, A. (2015). Cyberbullying: The discriminant factors among cyberbullies, cybervictims, and cyberbully-victims in a czech adolescent sample. *Journal of Interpersonal Violence, 30*(18), 3192–3216.

Blackwell, L. S., Trzesniewski, K. H. & Dweck, C. S. (2007). Implicit theories of intelligence predict achievement across an adolescent transition: A longitudinal study and an intervention. *Child Development, 78*(1), 246–263.

Boothby, E. J., Clark, M. S., & Bargh, J. A. (2014). Shared experiences are amplified. *Psychological Science, 25*(12), 2209–2216.

Breines, J. G., & Chen, S. (2012). Self-compassion increases self-improvement motivation. *Personality and Social Psychology Bulletin, 38*(9).

Brown, B. (2013). *Daring greatly: How the courage to be vulnerable transforms the way we live, love, parent and lead.* Vermilion.

Calhoun, C. D., Helms, S. W., Heilbron, N., Rudolph, K. D., Hastings, P. D., & Prinstein, M. J. (2014). Relational victimization, friendship, and adolescents' hypothalamic-pituitary-adrenal axis responses to an in vivo social stressor. *Developmental and Psychopathology, 26*(3), 605–618.

Campaert, K., Nocentini, A., & Menesini, E. (2018). The role of poor parenting and parental approval for children's moral disengagement. *Journal of Child and Family Studies, 27*(8), 2656–2667.

Casper, D. M., Card, N. A., & Barlow, C. (2020). Relational aggression and victimization during adolescence: A meta-analytic review of unique associations with popularity, peer acceptance, rejection, and friendship characteristics. *Journal of Adolescence, 80*, 41–52.

Choukas-Bradley, S., Sheppard, C. S., Prinstein, M. J., & Abela, J. R. (2019). A cross-cultural examination of peer status and social correlates in the United States and China. *Merrill-Palmer Quarterly, 65*(4), 423–446.

Clark, K. N., Dorio, N. B., Demaray, M. K., & Malecki, C. K. (2019). Understanding bullying, victimization, and bystander behaviors through resource control theory. *Child & Youth Care Forum, 49*(4), 489–510.

Coyne, S. M., Swit, C., Stockdale, L., & Summers, K. (2020). The growth of gossip: Socialization of relational aggression from adolescence to emerging adulthood. *Aggressive Behaviour, 46*(6), 535–546.

Csikszentmihalyi, M. (1999). If we are so rich, why aren't we happy? *American Psychologist, 54*(10), 821–827.

Darling Rasmussen, P., Storebo, O. J. & Lokkeholt, T., Voss, L. G., Shmueli-Goetz, Y, Bojesen, A. B., Simonsen, E, & Bilenberg, N. (2019). Attachment as a core feature of resilience: A systematic review and meta-analysis. *Psychological Reports, 122*(4), 1259–1296.

de Vries, R. E., Pronk, J., Olthof, T., & Goossens, F. A. (2020). Getting along and/or getting ahead: Differential HEXACO personality correlates of likeability and popularity among adolescents. *European Journal of Personality, 34*(2), 245–261.

Dunning, D. L., Griffiths, K., Kuyken, W., Crane, C., Foulkes, L., Parker, J., & Dalgleish, T. (2019). Research Review: The effects of mindfulness-based interventions on cognition and mental health in children and adolescents – a meta-analysis of randomized controlled trials. *Journal of Child Psychology and Psychiatry, and Allied Disciplines 60*(3), 244–258.

Dweck, C. (2017). *Mindset: Changing the Way You Think to Fulfil Your Potential.* Robinson.

Eisenberger, N. I., Lieberman, M. D. & Williams, K. D. (2003). Does rejection hurt? An FMRI study of social exclusion. *Science,* (302), 290–292.

Englander, E. (2020). *25 Myths about Bullying and Cyberbullying:* Wiley Blackwell.

Falla, D., Ortega-Ruiz, R., & Romera, E. M. (2021). Mechanisms of moral disengagement in the transition from cybergossip to cyberaggression: A longitudinal study. *International Journal Environ Res Public Health, 18*(3).

Feilhauer, J., & Cima, M. (2013). Youth psychopathy: Differential correlates of callous-unemotional traits, narcissism, and impulsivity. *Forensic Science Int, 224*(1-3), 1-7.

Flack, T. (2020). Relational aggression and relational inclusion in adolescents: the role of empathic concern for victims of relational aggression and perspective taking. *Emotional and Behavioural Difficulties, 25*(3-4), 201–214.

Frankl, V. (2008). *Man's Search for Meaning*: Random House UK.

Garrett, N., Lazzaro, S., Ariely, D. & Sharot, T. (2016). The brain adapts to dishonesty. *Nature Neuroscience, 19*, 1727–1732.

Gilbert, D. (2007). *Stumbling on Happiness*. Harper Perennial.

Guerin, N. & White, V. (2020). *ASSAD 2017 Statistics & Trends: Australian Secondary Students' Use of Tobacco, Alcohol, Over-the-counter Drugs, and Illicit Substances*. Second Edition. Cancer Council Victoria.

Gini, G., Thornberg, R., & Pozzoli, T. (2020). Individual moral disengagement and bystander behavior in bullying: The role of moral distress and collective moral disengagement. *Psychology of Violence, 10*(1), 38–47.

Giovannelli, I., Pacilli, M. G., Pagliaro, S., Tomasetto, C., & Barreto, M. (2017). Recalling an unfair experience reduces adolescents' dishonest behavioral intentions: The mediating role of justice sensitivity. *Social Justice Research, 31*(1), 23–40.

Hartl, A. C., Laursen, B., Cantin, S., & Vitaro, F. (2020). A test of the bistrategic control hypothesis of adolescent popularity. *Child Development, 91*(3), 635–648.

Hawley, P. H. (2003). Prosocial and coercive configurations of resource control in early adolescence: A case for the well-adapted Machiavellian. *Merrill-Palmer Quarterly, 49*(3), 279–309.

Hawley, P. H. (1999). The ontogenesis of social dominance: A strategy based evolutionary perspective. *Developmental Review, 19*, 97–132.

Hawley, P. H., Shorey, H. S., & Alderman, P. M. (2009). Attachment correlates of resource-control strategies: Possible origins of social dominance and interpersonal power differentials. *Journal of Social and Personal Relationships, 26*(8), 1097–1118.

Hodges, E. V., Boivin, M., Vitaro, F., & Bukowski, W. M. (1999). The power of friendship: protection against an escalating cycle of peer victimization. *Developmental Psychology, 35*(1), 94–101.

Jamal, F., Bonell, C., Harden, A., & Lorenc, T. (2015). The social ecology of girls' bullying practices: exploratory research in two London schools. *Sociology of Health and Illness, 37*(5), 731–744.

Jiang, Y., You, J., Hou, Y., Du, C., Lin, M. P., Zheng, X., & Ma, C. (2016). Buffering the effects of peer victimization on adolescent non-suicidal self-injury: The role of self-compassion and family cohesion. *Journal of Adolescence, 53*, 107–115.

Jones, S. C., & Magee, C. A. (2014). The role of family, friends and peers in Australian adolescent's alcohol consumption. *Drug and Alcohol Review, 33*(3), 304–313.

Juvonen, J., & Graham, S. (2014). Bullying in schools: the power of bullies and the plight of victims. *Annual Review of Psychology, 65*, 159–185.

Kleiser, M., & Mayeux, L. (2021). Popularity and gender prototypicality: An experimental approach. *Journal of Youth and Adolescence, 50*(1), 144–158.

Láng, A., & Birkás, B. (2015). Machiavellianism and parental attachment in adolescence. *SAGE Open, 5*(1).

Laninga-Wijnen, L., Harakeh, Z., Dijkstra, J. K., Veenstra, R., & Vollebergh, W. (2020). Who sets the aggressive popularity norm in classrooms? It's the number and strength of aggressive, prosocial, and bi-strategic adolescents. *Journal of Abnormal Child Psychology, 48*(1), 13–27.

Lau, K. S. L., Marsee, M. A., Lapré, G. E., & Halmos, M. B. (2016). Does parental relational aggression interact with parental psychological control in the prediction of youth relational aggression? *Deviant Behavior, 37*(8), 904–916.

Lereya, S. T., Samara, M., & Wolke, D. (2013). Parenting behavior and the risk of becoming a victim and a bully/victim: a meta-analysis study. *Child Abuse & Neglect, 37*(12), 1091–1108.

Lim, M. H., Lonely in lockdown? You're not alone. 1 in 2 Australians feel more lonely since coronavirus. *The Conversation, July 2020*

Lim, M. H., Eres, R., Peck, C. (2019). *The Young Australian Loneliness Survey: Understanding Loneliness in Adolescents and Young Adults.* Swinburne University Technology VicHealth.

Mangels, J. A., Butterfield, B., Lamb, J., Good, C., & Dweck, C. S. (2006). Why do beliefs about intelligence influence learning success? A social cognitive neuroscience model. *Social Cognitive Affective Neuroscience, 1*(2), 75–86.

Massey, K., Burns, J., & Franz, A. (2021). Young people, sexuality and the age of pornography. *Sexuality & Culture, 25*(1), 318–336.

Mas-Tur, A., Tur-Porcar, A., & Llorca, A. (2016). Social media marketing for adolescents. *Psychology & Marketing, 33*(12), 1119–1125.

Menesini, E., & Salmivalli, C. (2017). Bullying in schools: the state of knowledge and effective interventions. *Psychology, Health and Medicine, 22*(sup1), 240–253.

Mogilner, C. (2010). The pursuit of happiness: time, money and social connections. *Psychological Science, 21*(9), 1348–1354.

Neff, K. D. (2003). Development and validation of a scale to measure self-compassion. *Self and Identity, 2,* 223–250.

Neff, K. (2015). *Self-Compassion: The Proven Power of Being Kind to Yourself.* HarperCollins Publishers.

Neff, K. (2021). *Fierce Self-Compassion : How Women Can Harness Kindness to Speak Up, Claim Their Power, and Thrive.* Penguin Books Ltd.

Nesi, J., & Prinstein, M. J. (2015). Using social media for social comparison and feedback-seeking: Gender and popularity moderate associations with depressive symptoms. *Journal of Abnormal Child Psychology, 43*(8), 1427–1438.

Niemiec, C. P., Ryan, R. M., & Deci, E. L. (2009). The path taken: Consequences of attaining intrinsic and extrinsic aspirations in post-college Life. *Journal of Research in Personality, 73*(3), 291–306.

Ormerod, A. J., Collinsworth, L. L., & Perry, L. A. (2008). Critical climate: Relations among sexual harassment, climate and outcomes for high school girls and boys. *Psychology of Women Quarterly, 32,* 113–125.

Padgett, S., & Notar, C. E. (2013). Bystanders are the key to stopping bullying. *Universal Journal of Educational Research, 1*(2), 33–41.

Palmer, J. A., & Tackett, S. (2018). An examination of the dark triad constructs with regard to prosocial behavior. *Acta Psychopathologica, 04*(01).

Peterson, C., Park, N., Pole, N., D'Andrea, W., & Seligman, M. E. (2008). Strengths of character and posttraumatic growth. *Journal of Traumatic Stress, 21*(2), 214-217.

Pozzoli, T., Gini, G., & Thornberg, R. (2017). Getting angry matters: Going beyond perspective taking and empathic concern to understand bystanders' behavior in bullying. *Journal of Adolescence, 61,* 87–95.

Prinstein, M. J. (2017). *Popular.* Viking.

Prinstein, M. J., & Wargo Aikins, J. (2004). Cognitive moderators of the longitudinal association between peer rejection and adolescent depressive symptoms. *Journal of Abnormal Child Psychology, 32*(2), 147–158.

Prinstein, M. J. & Cilessen, A. (2003). Forms and function of adolescent peer aggression associated with high levels of peer status. *Merrill-Palmer Quarterly, 49*(3).

Reijntjes, A., Vermande, M., Thomaes, S., Goossens, F., Olthof, T., Aleva, L., & Van der Meulen, M. (2016). Narcissism, bullying, and social dominance in youth: A longitudinal analysis. *Journal of Abnormal Child Psychology, 44*(1), 63–74.

Rockwell, D. & Giles, D. (2009). Being a celebrity: A phenomenology of fame. *Journal of Phenomenological Psychology, 40*(2), 178–210.

Romera, E. M., Casas, J. A., Gómez-Ortiz, O., & Ortega-Ruiz, R. (2019). Moral domain as a risk and protective factor against bullying. An integrating perspective review on the complexity of morality. *Aggression and Violent Behavior, 45*, 75–82.

Runions, K. C., Salmivalli, C., Shaw, T., Burns, S., & Cross, D. (2018). Beyond the reactive-proactive dichotomy: Rage, revenge, reward, and recreational aggression predict early high school bully and bully/victim status. *Aggressive Behavior, 44*(7).

Salzberg, S. (2020). *Real Change: Mindfulness to Heal Ourselves and the World.* Flatiron Books.

Salzberg, S., & Thurman, R. (2013). *Love Your Enemies: How to Break the Anger Habit and be a Whole Lot Happier.* Hay House.

Santos, L. (2021) *The science of wellbeing by Yale University.* Coursera.

Schutte, N. S., & Malouff, J. M. (2019). The impact of signature character strengths interventions: A meta-analysis. *Journal of Happiness Studies, 20*(4), 1179–1196.

Seligman, M. (2004). *Authentic Happiness: A Visionary New Understanding of Happiness and Wellbeing.* Free Press.

Seligman, M. (2011). *Flourish: A visionary new understanding of happiness and wellbeing.* Atria.

Sherman, L. E., Payton, A. A., Hernandez, L. M., Greenfield, P. M., & Dapretto, M. (2016). The power of the like in adolescence: Effects of peer influence on neural and behavioral responses to social media. *Psychological Science, 27*(7), 1027–1035.

Siegel, D. J., & Payne Bryson, T. (2011). *The Whole-Brain Child: 12 Revolutionary Strategies to Nurture Your Child's Developing Mind, Survive Everyday Parenting Struggles, and Help Your Family Thrive*. Delacorte Press

Stanley, N., Barter, C., Wood, M., Aghtaie, N., Larkins, C., Lanau, A., & Overlien, C. (2018). Pornography, sexual coercion and abuse and sexting in young people's intimate relationships: A European study. *Journal of Interpersonal Violence, 33*(19), 2919–2944.

Stefan, D., Lefdahl-Davis, E. M., Alayan, A. J., Decker, M., Kulwicki, T. M., Parsell, J. S., & Wittwer, J. L. (2021). The impact of gratitude letters and visits on relationships, happiness, wellbeing and meaning of graduate students. *Journal of Applied School Psychology, 5*(2), 1–17.

Strecher, V. (Producer). (2021). *Finding Purpose and Meaning in Life: Living for What Matters Most*. University of Michigan.

Suh, H., & Jeong, J. (2021). Association of self-compassion with suicidal thoughts and behaviors and non-suicidal self injury: A meta-analysis. *Frontiers in Psychology, 12.*

Tatkin, S. (2016). *Wired for Dating: How Understanding Neurobiology and Attachment Style Can Help You Find Your Ideal Mate*. New Harbinger Publications.

Thomas, S. E. (2017). "What should I do?": Young women's reported dilemmas with nude photographs. *Sexuality Research and Social Policy, 15*(2), 192–207.

Thornberg, R., Wänström, L., Elmelid, R., Johansson, A., & Mellander, E. (2020). Standing up for the victim or supporting the bully? Bystander responses and their associations with moral disengagement, defender self-efficacy, and collective efficacy. *Social Psychology of Education, 23*(3), 563–581.

Twenge, J. M., & Campbell, W. K. (2009). *The Narcissism Epidemic: Living in the Age of Entitlement*. Free Press.

Twenge, J. M., Campbell, W. K., & Freeman, E. C. (2012). Generational differences in young adults' life goals, concern for others, and civic orientation, 1966-2009. *Journal of Personality and Social Psychology, 102*(5), 1045–1062.

Twenge, J. M., & Farley, E. (2021). Not all screen time is created equal: associations with mental health vary by activity and gender. *Social Psychiatry and Psychiatric Epidemiology, 56*(2), 207–217.

Tydén, T., & Rogala, C. (2004). Sexual behaviour among young men in Sweden and the impact of pornography. *International Journal of STD and AIDS, 15,* 590–693.

Vaillant, G. E. (2015). *Triumphs of Experience: The Harvard Grant Study*: Harvard University Press.

Valido, A., Ingram, K., Espelage, D. L., Torgal, C., Merrin, G. J., & Davis, J. P. (2020). Intra-familial violence and peer aggression among early adolescents: Moderating role of school sense of belonging. *Journal of Family Violence, 36*(1), 87–98.

van Geel, M., Toprak, F., Goemans, A., Zwaanswijk, W., & Vedder, P. (2016). Are youth psychopathic traits related to bullying? Meta-analyses on callous-unemotional traits, narcissism, and impulsivity. *Child Psychiatry and Human Development, 48*(5), 768–777.

Vandenbosch, L., & Eggermont, S. (2016). The interrelated roles of mass media and social media in adolescents' development of an objectified self-concept. *Communication Research, 43*(8), 1116–1140.

Vazeou-Nieuwenhuis, A., & Schumann, K. (2018). Self-compassionate and apologetic? How and why having compassion toward the self relates to a willingness to apologize. *Personality and Individual Differences, 124*, 71–76.

Vigna, A. J., Poehlmann-Tynan, J., & Koenig, B. W. (2020). Is self-compassion protective among sexual- and gender-minority adolescents across racial groups? *Mindfulness, 11*(3), 800–815.

Vogel, E. A., Rose, J. P., Roberts, L. R., & Eckles, K. (2014). Social comparison, social media, and self-esteem. *Psychology of Popular Media Culture, 3*(4), 206–222.

Waldinger, R. (2015). *What makes a good life? Lessons from the longest study on happiness.* TEDxBeaconStreet

Walker, B. (1991). *Eat, My Fine Coat.* Teaching Tolerance, Southern Poverty Law Center, Retrieved from https://www.learningforjustice.org/classroom-resources/texts/eat-my-fine-coat.

Wang, X., Wang, W., Qiao, Y., Gao, L., Yang, J., & Wang, P. (2020). Parental phubbing and adolescents' cyberbullying perpetration: A moderated mediation model of moral disengagement and online disinhibition. *Journal of Interpersonal Violence, 1-23*

Wang, X., Yang, J., Wang, P., & Lei, L. (2019). Childhood maltreatment, moral disengagement, and adolescents' cyberbullying perpetration: Fathers' and mothers' moral disengagement as moderators. *Computers in Human Behavior, 95*, 48–57.

Ware, B. (2019). *The Top Five Regrets of the Dying: A Life Transformed by the Dearly Departing.* Hay House.

Wargo Aikins, J., Collibee, C., & Cunningham, J. (2016). Gossiping to the top. *The Journal of Early Adolescence, 37*(5), 642–661.

Wong, G. T. W., & Manning, M. (2017). Adolescent illicit drug use and policy options in Australia: A multicriteria decision analysis. *Journal of Drug Issues, 47*(4), 638–664.

Young, J., E., Klosko, J. S., & Weishaar, M. E. (2003). *Schema Therapy: A Practitioner's Guide.* The Guilford Press.

Zhang, X., Pomerantz, E. M., Qin, L., Logis, H., Ryan, A. M., & Wang, M. (2018). Characteristics of likability, perceived popularity, and admiration in the early adolescent peer system in the United States and China. *Developmental Psychology, 54*(8), 1568–1581.

Zych, I., Gómez-Ortiz, O., Fernández Touceda, L., Nasaescu, E., & Llorent, V. J. (2020). Parental moral disengagement induction as a predictor of bullying and cyberbullying: Mediation by children's moral disengagement, moral emotions, and validation of a questionnaire. *Child Indicators Research, 13*(3), 1065–1083.